## Standard Grade | Credit

# French

Leckie×Leckie

First exam published in 2002.

Published by Leckie & Leckie Ltd, 3rd Floor, 4 Queen Street, Edinburgh EH2 1JE

tel: 0131 220 6831 fax: 0131 225 9987 enquiries@leckieandleckie.co.uk www.leckieandleckie.co.uk

ISBN 1-84372-399-9   ISBN-13 978-1-84372-399-8

A CIP Catalogue record for this book is available from the British Library.

Printed in Scotland by Scotprint.

Leckie & Leckie is a division of Granada Learning Limited.

Leckie & Leckie is grateful to the copyright holders, as credited at the back of the book, for permission to use their material. Every effort has been made to trace the copyright holders and to obtain their permission for the use of copyright material. Leckie & Leckie will gladly receive information enabling them to rectify any error or omission in subsequent editions.

**[BLANK PAGE]**

C

**1000/403**

NATIONAL
QUALIFICATIONS
2002

WEDNESDAY, 15 MAY
11.10 AM – 12.10 PM

FRENCH
STANDARD GRADE
Credit Level
Reading

**Instructions to the Candidate**

When you are told to do so, open your paper and write your answers **in English** in the **separate** answer book provided.

You may use a French dictionary.

SCOTTISH
QUALIFICATIONS
AUTHORITY

©

*Marks*

**1.** You find this article about the environment in a magazine.

Les problèmes de l'environnement, c'est à qui de les résoudre? A l'individu, ou aux gouvernements?

A mon avis, respecter l'environnement et le protéger, c'est le problème de tout le monde. C'est notre monde à nous et nous devons le défendre, parce que, si nous ne le défendons pas, personne ne le fera à notre place. Si seulement chacun de nous faisait un petit geste comme jeter ses déchets à la poubelle, les villes seraient bien plus propres. Mais il faut sensibiliser les personnes de tous les pays, de tous les âges. Si on encourageait tout le monde à respecter un peu mieux son environnement, on n'aurait pas à se poser la question de l'écologie!

(*a*) Why are environmental problems a matter for everyone? Mention **one** thing.

1

(*b*) What can the individual do? How would this help?

2

(*c*) People must be made aware of the situation. What should they be urged to do?

1

**2.** The article continues.

Mais ce n'est pas seulement l'individu qui doit penser aux dangers: les gouvernements de tous les pays du monde devraient créer de nouvelles lois, et être plus sévères. Par exemple, il faudrait des policiers dans les rues pour surveiller les piétons. Quelqu'un qui jette un papier ou même un mégot par terre devrait payer une amende.

Le problème de la pollution de la Terre a vraiment une importance mondiale. Les pays doivent tous oublier leurs différences et se mettre ensemble pour trouver une solution. Sinon, on risque à la fin de tout détruire.

(*a*) The police could be involved in tackling the problem. In what way would this be done? Mention **two** things.

2

(*b*) Pollution is an international problem. What does the author say must be done? Why?

2

*Marks*

**3.** Some young people are talking about marriage.

Beaucoup de jeunes pensent que le mariage est une institution dépassée, quelque chose d'un autre temps, qui n'est plus nécessaire. A leur avis, si deux personnes s'aiment vraiment, cet amour peut durer toute la vie. On n'a pas besoin d'un contrat qui est simplement une feuille de papier! En tout cas, ce contrat n'est pas toujours respecté. Ils parlent du grand nombre de divorces, qui augmente chaque année. Aussi, beaucoup de couples vivent ensemble, tout heureux, sans se marier.

Il y a aussi des couples qui ne sont ni pour ni contre le mariage, mais qui ont peut-être l'intention de se marier plus tard dans la vie. S'ils décident d'avoir une famille, le mariage permet d'avoir un lien légal et une reconnaissance sociale. Ça peut avoir de l'importance pour les enfants.

*(a)* Many young people think that marriage is outdated. What reasons are given for this? Mention any **two** things.

2

*(b)* Why do some people decide to get married later on? Mention any **three** things.

3

**4.** The article goes on.

D'après beaucoup de gens, le mariage est seulement pour les couples romantiques ou religieux. Quant à la religion, il y a deux points de vue: pour certains le mariage est fait pour montrer d'abord à Dieu et aussi à ses amis qu'on a trouvé le bon partenaire; pour d'autres la cérémonie religieuse n'est qu'un rituel, n'est qu'une tradition. Mais il y a aussi des gens pour qui la tradition est très importante. Pour eux, la cérémonie de mariage annonce le commencement d'une nouvelle vie! Ça fait partie d'une journée inoubliable, avec une belle robe blanche, une grande fête et des cadeaux.

Qui a raison? Qui sait? Chacun a droit à son point de vue!

*(a)* Two different points of view regarding the religious ceremony of marriage are mentioned. What are they?

2

*(b)* The traditional ceremony is important to some people. Why? Mention any **two** things.

2

*Marks*

**5.** A group of young people are talking about clothes and fashion.

La question de vêtements est toujours intéressante. Voici les opinions de quelques jeunes Français:

**Patrice**: En m'habillant, j'indique mon style et aussi le groupe moderne et sportif auquel j'appartiens. Pour moi, *les fringues* reflètent ma personnalité et mon humeur: quand je suis triste, je m'habille en couleurs sombres—noir, bleu marine, beige, gris—et puis le lendemain, ma tristesse passée, c'est les fringues multicolores que je mets. Quand je me sens un peu déprimé, je sors les grands pulls et quand je suis en forme je mets des vêtements chic. J'attache beaucoup d'importance à ce que je porte et j'y consacre la moitié de mon budget.

* les fringues (slang) — clothes

(a) Patrice believes he shows his personality through what he wears. How does he show what mood he is in? Mention any **two** things.　　2

(b) What tells us that he thinks clothes are important?　　1

**6.** Claudine gives her views on fashion.

**Claudine**: Moi, je ne me cache pas derrière la mode, je ne me montre pas trop non plus. Pour moi, c'est pas grand'chose! Je veux tout simplement me sentir à l'aise dans mes vêtements, donc je m'habille comme je veux avec ce qui me plaît. Si ce n'est pas la dernière mode, si mes copains n'aiment pas, ça, c'est leur problème. Je préfère dépenser mon argent sur des choses que je trouve plus importantes: les sorties, les jeux vidéo, la musique.

Claudine thinks that fashion is not important. How does she explain her attitude? Mention any **three** things.　　3

**7.** Laure states her point of view regarding fashion.

*Marks*

> **Laure**: Eh bien, je n'ai pas beaucoup d'argent moi, alors ce que je porte doit être pratique et pas trop cher. Donc, c'est le jean. Pourquoi? D'abord, le jean est facile à laver, et on peut porter toutes sortes de choses avec, (par exemple une chemise élégante ou un simple tee-shirt), mais pour moi le plus important c'est que je peux en porter sans avoir peur de me ridiculiser. En plus, je ne veux pas être différente de mes copains.

According to Laure, jeans are practical and inexpensive. What are her other reasons for wearing jeans? Mention any **three** things.

3

**Total (26)**

*[END OF QUESTION PAPER]*

[BLANK PAGE]

C

# 1000/409

NATIONAL
QUALIFICATIONS
2002

WEDNESDAY, 15 MAY
2.30 PM – 3.00 PM
(APPROX.)

## FRENCH
## STANDARD GRADE
Credit Level
Listening Transcript

**This paper must not be seen by any candidate.**

The material overleaf is provided for use in an emergency only (eg the tape or equipment proving faulty) or where permission has been given in advance by SQA for the material to be read to candidates with special needs.  The material must be read exactly as printed.

## Transcript—Credit Level

> **Instructions to reader(s):**
>
> For each item, read the English **once,** then read the French **three times**, with an interval of 5 seconds between the readings. On completion of the third reading, pause for the length of time indicated in brackets after each item, to allow the candidates to write their answers.
>
> Where special arrangements have been agreed in advance to allow the reading of the material, those sections marked **(f)** should be read by a female speaker and those marked **(m)** by a male: those sections marked **(t)** should be read by the teacher.

**(t)** You hear Antoine and his sister Christine talking about how having a Scottish father has influenced their lives so far. Antoine is the first to speak and he introduces himself.

**(m)**     **Bonjour, je m'appelle Antoine et j'habite en Dordogne.**

**(t) Question number one.**

What does his father do? Mention any **one** thing.

**(m)**     **Mon père travaille le bois. Il fabrique des tables, des meubles et d'autres choses comme ça.**

*(40 seconds)*

**(t) Question number two.**

Where did his parents meet?

**(m)**     **Mes parents se sont rencontrés sur le bateau entre l'Angleterre et la France. Ils sont vite tombés amoureux.**

*(40 seconds)*

**(t) Question number three.**

Antoine talks about the time when he and his family lived in Scotland.

What does he say? Mention any **three** things.

**(m)**     **J'ai vécu en Ecosse trois mois seulement. Mes parents avaient échangé leur maison avec de très bons amis. Ma soeur allait à l'école en Ecosse, mais moi, j'étais encore trop jeune.**

*(40 seconds)*

**(t) Question number four.**

He talks about his impressions of Scotland.  He compares Scottish eating habits with those in France.

What does he say?  Mention **two** things.

**(m)**      **Je n'aime pas les déjeuners qui consistent en un sandwich, un paquet de chips et une boisson gazeuse et beaucoup d'Ecossais ne mangent que ça.  Par contre, en France, nous avons l'habitude de manger un grand repas à midi.**

*(40 seconds)*

**(t) Question number five.**

How do his views on Scottish weather differ from those of most people?

**(m)**      **J'aime l'Ecosse, mais comme dans tous les pays il y a des avantages et des inconvénients. La plupart des personnes trouvent le climat très dur en Ecosse.  Moi, cela ne me dérange pas.  J'aime la pluie et j'adore le vent.**

*(40 seconds)*

**(t) Question number six.**

Why did his parents finally choose to settle in France rather than in Scotland?  Mention any **two** things.

**(m)**      **Mes parents ont décidé de vivre en France car ils aimaient beaucoup le mode de vie français.  Ils ont découvert que la vie était beaucoup plus simple, qu'ils avaient beaucoup de liberté, et que tout le monde était moins stressé.**

*(40 seconds)*

**(t) Question number seven.**

Antoine's sister Christine then talks about her experiences.  According to her, why did the family go to live in New Zealand for six months?  Mention any **three** things.

**(f)**      **On est allé vivre en Nouvelle-Zélande parce qu'on habitait depuis quinze ans dans le même petit village en Dordogne.  Mes parents ont décidé qu'ils avaient besoin d'un changement. Ils voulaient voyager et voir le monde.  Il y avait aussi la possibilité de faire des progrès en anglais.**

*(40 seconds)*

**(t) Question number eight.**

What did their parents have to do before they could go to New Zealand?  Mention any **one** thing.

What made things easier for them?

**(f)**      **Avant de partir, mes parents ont dû faire des économies pendant plusieurs années.  Ils ont dû trouver une école là-bas pour mon frère et moi.  Ce n'était pas facile.  Heureusement, nous avions une amie qui nous a trouvé un appartement à Wellington, la capitale de la Nouvelle-Zélande.**

*(40 seconds)*

**[Turn over for Questions 9 to 11 on *Page four***

**(t) Question number nine.**

What did they do first in New Zealand?

How were they able to cope financially?  Mention **two** things.

**(f)**        En Nouvelle-Zélande, nous avons passé le premier mois à voyager à travers tout le pays. Puis, nous nous sommes installés à Wellington où ma mère donnait des leçons de musique.  Mon père travaillait comme jardinier pour gagner un peu d'argent.

*(40 seconds)*

**(t) Question number ten.**

According to Christine, school in New Zealand compared favourably with school in France.  Give any **four** reasons why.

**(f)**        L'école, c'était super.  Les professeurs écoutaient et s'intéressaient à chaque élève, et ils donnaient des cours intéressants.  Les élèves étaient beaucoup plus libres et les cours commençaient plus tard et finissaient plus tôt qu'en France.

*(40 seconds)*

**(t) Question number eleven.**

What impressed Christine most about New Zealand?  Mention any **two** things.

**(f)**        Ce qui m'a le plus impressionnée, c'est la beauté de la nature et le fait que chaque Néo-Zélandais respecte son environnement.  Tout est propre.  C'est à dire qu'il y a très peu d'ordures, très peu de papiers dans la rue.

*(40 seconds)*

**(t) End of test.**

**Now look over your answers.**

*[END OF TRANSCRIPT]*

C

## 1000/408

NATIONAL QUALIFICATIONS 2002

WEDNESDAY, 15 MAY 2.30 PM – 3.00 PM (APPROX.)

FRENCH STANDARD GRADE
Credit Level
Listening

**Instructions to the Candidate**

When you are told to do so, open your paper.

You will hear a number of short items in French. You will hear each item three times, then you will have time to write your answer.

Write your answers, **in English**, in the **separate** answer book provided.

You may take notes as you are listening to the French, but only in your answer book.

You may **not** use a French dictionary.

You are not allowed to leave the examination room until the end of the test.

SCOTTISH
QUALIFICATIONS
AUTHORITY

©

*Marks*

You hear Antoine and his sister Christine talking about how having a Scottish father has influenced their lives so far. Antoine is the first to speak and he introduces himself.

Bonjour, je m'appelle Antoine et j'habite en Dordogne.

1. What does his father do? Mention any **one** thing.                                  1

\* \* \* \* \*

2. Where did his parents meet?                                                          1

\* \* \* \* \*

3. Antoine talks about the time when he and his family lived in Scotland.

   What does he say? Mention any **three** things.                                      3

\* \* \* \* \*

4. He talks about his impressions of Scotland. He compares Scottish eating habits with those in France.

   What does he say? Mention **two** things.                                            2

\* \* \* \* \*

5. How do his views on Scottish weather differ from those of most people?              2

\* \* \* \* \*

6. Why did his parents finally choose to settle in France rather than in Scotland? Mention any **two** things.                                                            2

\* \* \* \* \*

7. Antoine's sister Christine then talks about her experiences. According to her, why did the family go to live in New Zealand for six months? Mention any **three** things.                                                                   3

\* \* \* \* \*

8. (*a*) What did their parents have to do before they could go to New Zealand? Mention any **one** thing.                                                         1

   (*b*) What made things easier for them?                                              1

\* \* \* \* \*

*Marks*

9.  (*a*)  What did they do first in New Zealand?  **1**

    (*b*)  How were they able to cope financially?  Mention **two** things.  **2**

\*　　\*　　\*　　\*　　\*

10.  According to Christine, school in New Zealand compared favourably with school in France.  Give any **four** reasons why.  **4**

\*　　\*　　\*　　\*　　\*

11.  What impressed Christine most about New Zealand?  Mention any **two** things.  **2**

\*　　\*　　\*　　\*　　\*

**Total (25)**

*[END OF QUESTION PAPER]*

[BLANK PAGE]

**[BLANK PAGE]**

FOR OFFICIAL USE

C

Total Marks

# 1000/403

NATIONAL
QUALIFICATIONS
2003

WEDNESDAY, 14 MAY
11.10 AM – 12.10 PM

**FRENCH**
STANDARD GRADE
Credit Level
Reading

---

**Fill in these boxes and read what is printed below.**

Full name of centre

Town

Forename(s)

Surname

Date of birth
Day  Month  Year

Scottish candidate number

Number of seat

When you are told to do so, open your paper and write your answers **in English** in the spaces provided.

You may use a French dictionary.

Before leaving the examination room you must give this book to the invigilator. If you do not, you may lose all the marks for this paper.

SCOTTISH
QUALIFICATIONS
AUTHORITY

©

**1.**   You read this article about working hours in France.

---

## Le Temps de Travail en France – un peu d'histoire

**1900**: Une loi réduit le temps de travail à dix heures par jour.

**1906**: Fin du travail sept jours sur sept. Le dimanche est jour de repos obligatoire.

**1919**: La durée du travail ne doit pas dépasser huit heures par jour.

**1936**: La durée du travail est fixée à quarante heures par semaine, avec, pour la première fois, deux semaines de congés payés par an.

**1981**: Le travail est limité à trente-neuf heures par semaine, avec cinq semaines de congés payés.

---

Complete these sentences:                                                                              **3**

In 1900 the working day _____ .

In 1906 Sunday became a _____ .

In 1936 people were given _____ per year.

**[Turn over for Question 2 on *Page four***

DO NO
WRITE
THIS
MARGI

*Marks*

**2.** The article goes on to talk about the latest development in working hours in France.

---

## Pour créer davantage d'emplois – il faut partager le travail

Aujourd'hui en France, plus de 3 millions, dont 700 000 jeunes de moins de 25 ans, sont sans travail.

Pour combattre ce chômage, le gouvernement propose de limiter le temps de travail à 35 heures par semaine au lieu de 39 heures actuellement. Cela permettrait de faire travailler davantage de personnes. Selon les calculs des experts, le passage de 39 à 35 heures pourrait créer jusqu'à 1,5 million d'emplois en cinq ans.

En travaillant moins, on gagne moins d'argent. Pourtant, d'après un récent sondage du journal «Le Monde», près de 70% des Français accepteraient une légère baisse de salaire pour travailler moins et permettre la création de nouveaux emplois.

Mais, partager le travail demande aussi de changer l'organisation des entreprises, et certains patrons pensent que cela est trop compliqué et trop coûteux.

Au mois d'octobre, le gouvernement, les travailleurs et les chefs d'entreprise se rencontrent pour essayer de trouver une solution.

---

(a) What figures are given about unemployment in France? Mention **two** things.

2

_____

_____

_____

(b) How does the French government intend to tackle this problem?

1

_____

_____

(c) According to the survey in *Le Monde*, what has been the response of most French people to the proposal?

2

_____

_____

_____

*Marks*

**2.** **(continued)**

(*d*)  Which group of people is not so keen on the proposal?  Why?                    **2**

_____

_____

_____

(*e*)  What is to happen in October?                    **1**

_____

_____

**[Turn over**

**3.** You read an article about what houses will be like in the future.

*Marks*

---

### LA MAISON DU FUTUR

La technologie avance si vite. Qu'est-ce qu'on trouvera dans la maison de l'an 2020? Dans cette maison, un micro est relié à l'ordinateur qui contrôle toutes les fonctions de la maison.

**La cuisine**:

C'est un vrai paradis! Quand on a faim, on dit ce qu'on veut manger, et l'ordinateur donne non seulement la liste des ingrédients, mais aussi la méthode et le temps de cuisson. Et en plus, il allume la cuisinière et contrôle la température du four.

Le soir, en rentrant du travail, on envoie un message électronique directement de sa voiture à l'ordinateur. Et voilà! Un plat chaud sera prêt quand on arrivera!

### Le frigo:

Dès qu'on prend du lait, du fromage ou d'autres produits dans le frigo, l'ordinateur enregistre les codes-barres. Il note constamment le contenu du frigo, envoie des commandes au supermarché et puis le commerçant livre ce qui manque.

---

*(a)* A microphone will be connected to the "house" computer. What will happen when you tell the computer what you want to eat? Mention any **three** things.

**3**

_____

_____

_____

_____

*(b)* You are travelling home from work. How will you be sure of a hot meal when you arrive home?

**1**

_____

_____

*(c)* What will happen when you take something out of the fridge? Mention any **three** things.

**3**

_____

_____

_____

_____

*Marks*

**4.** The article continues.

**La salle de bains**:

On commande son bain de n'importe quelle pièce de la maison. Par une télécommande mobile, on programme l'heure du bain et la température de l'eau. La baignoire se remplit automatiquement. On n'a qu'à plonger dedans.

**Le cinéma à la maison**:

On commande le film qu'on veut, et on le voit comme au cinéma. Le mur du salon devient un écran géant et il y a des haut-parleurs dans tous les coins de la pièce.

**Dans la chambre**:

C'est l'heure de se coucher. On se met au lit et l'ordinateur règle le matelas selon la position qu'on prend. On n'aura plus jamais mal au dos!

(*a*) Why will it be easy to take a bath in this house of the future? Mention any **two** things.

2

_____

_____

_____

(*b*) Watching a film at home will be just like going to the cinema. Why? Mention **two** things.

2

_____

_____

_____

(*c*) Why will you always get a good night's sleep?

1

_____

_____

**[Turn over for Question 5 on *Page eight***

*Marks*

**5.** You read an article about passports for animals.

**Un passeport pour animaux.**

Les animaux ont aussi leur passeport! Depuis cent ans, les chats et les chiens entrant au Royaume-Uni doivent passer six mois au chenil afin d'éviter l'importation de toute maladie. Maintenant en Angleterre, pour échapper au chenil, on peut implanter une puce électronique sur les animaux. Elle permet de vérifier la provenance et l'état physique de l'animal.

(*a*) Why did cats and dogs have to spend time in quarantine before entering the UK?

1

_____

_____

(*b*) What information will be carried by the electronic implant? Mention **two** things.

2

_____

_____

_____

**Total (26)**

[*END OF QUESTION PAPER*]

C

**1000/409**

NATIONAL
QUALIFICATIONS
2003

WEDNESDAY, 14 MAY
2.30 PM – 3.00 PM
(APPROX.)

FRENCH
STANDARD GRADE
Credit Level
Listening Transcript

**This paper must not be seen by any candidate.**

The material overleaf is provided for use in an emergency only (eg the CD or equipment proving faulty) or where permission has been given in advance by SQA for the material to be read to candidates with special needs. The material must be read exactly as printed.

SCOTTISH
QUALIFICATIONS
AUTHORITY

**Transcript—Credit Level**

---

**Instructions to reader(s):**

For each item, read the English **once,** then read the French **three times**, with an interval of 5 seconds between the readings. On completion of the third reading, pause for the length of time indicated in brackets after each item, to allow the candidates to write their answers.

Where special arrangements have been agreed in advance to allow the reading of the material, those sections marked **(f)** should be read by a female speaker and those marked **(m)** by a male: those sections marked **(t)** should be read by the teacher.

---

**(t)** You hear a radio interview with Richard Giraud, a fifteen year old French boy who recently took part in an interesting, but unusual exchange.

**(m)**       **Vous écoutez une interview avec Richard Giraud, un jeune Français de quinze ans, qui a récemment participé à un échange intéressant, mais pas vraiment typique.**

**(t) Question number one.**

Richard lives with his parents on a farm.

What makes his lifestyle lonely? Mention any **two** things.

**(m)**       **Je suis enfant unique. J'habite avec mes parents dans une petite ferme à vingt-deux kilomètres de la ville. La ferme est très isolée, donc nous recevons rarement des visites.**

*(40 seconds)*

**(t) Question number two.**

What is his normal morning routine? Mention any **two** things.

**(m)**       **En semaine, je me lève à six heures moins le quart. Je dois aider mon père avec les vaches avant de manger rapidement et de prendre l'autocar pour aller au lycée en ville.**

*(40 seconds)*

**(t) Question number three.**

What does he do when he gets home from school?

Why does he go to bed early? Mention any **one** thing.

**(m)**       **Le soir, en rentrant, j'ai toujours mes devoirs à faire. D'habitude, je me couche tôt parce que je suis souvent fatigué et je dois me lever tôt le lendemain.**

*(40 seconds)*

**(t) Question number four.**

Why are Richard's parents sometimes concerned about him?

Describe the exchange they organised for him. Mention **two** things.

**(m)** Parfois, mes parents s'inquiètent pour moi. A part mes amis au lycée, j'ai peu de contact avec des gens de mon âge; donc, mes parents ont organisé un échange. Je suis allé passer un mois chez mon camarade de classe, Pierre, qui habite en ville. Pendant que je logeais chez sa famille, Pierre est venu vivre chez nous à la ferme.

*(40 seconds)*


**(t) Question number five.**

What problem did Richard have at the beginning of the exchange?

Why was this? Mention any **one** thing.

**(m)** Au début, je ne dormais pas bien. Il n'y avait plus le calme de la campagne. Pendant la nuit, j'entendais tous les bruits de la rue—les gens qui rentraient tard et les voitures qui passaient.

*(40 seconds)*


**(t) Question number six.**

What was he now able to do after school? Mention any **two** things.

What information does he give about a school trip? Mention **two** things.

**(m)** Après les cours, je sortais avec mes copains. Nous sommes allés voir des films, nous avons bavardé au café et, le week-end, nous sommes rentrés très tard après la discothèque. J'ai même participé à une sortie scolaire avec notre professeur de biologie. Nous sommes allés étudier les petits animaux qui vivent sur les bords d'une rivière.

*(40 seconds)*


**(t) Question number seven.**

During the exchange, Richard met his girlfriend, Véronique.

Where did they meet?

What does he say about Véronique? Mention any **two** things.

**(m)** Mais, le plus important, c'est que j'ai maintenant une petite amie. Elle s'appelle Véronique et je l'ai rencontrée chez un copain qui fêtait son anniversaire. Elle s'intéresse beaucoup aux animaux et elle veut devenir vétérinaire. Bientôt, elle vient passer un week-end chez nous à la ferme.

*(40 seconds)*


**[Turn over for Questions 8 to 10 on *Page four***

**(t) Question number eight.**

Véronique is hoping to go to university soon.

Why does she not enjoy school life? Mention **two** things.

**(f)** **Quitter le lycée après le bac et aller à l'université, ça, c'est mon rêve. Je n'aime pas du tout ma vie d'élève au lycée. D'abord, je ne m'entends pas bien avec les profs; et puis, je dois assister à des cours qui sont vraiment ennuyeux, par exemple l'histoire.**

*(40 seconds)*

**(t) Question number nine.**

What does she say about her part-time job? Mention any **two** things.

**(f)** **Le week-end je travaille dans un grand magasin. Le travail n'est pas trop dur, mais ce n'est pas bien payé, donc je ne gagne pas l'argent nécessaire pour sortir avec les copains le soir.**

*(40 seconds)*

**(t) Question number ten.**

Véronique is looking forward to student life.

Why? Mention **three** things.

**(f)** **La vie d'étudiante m'attire beaucoup. J'aurai beaucoup plus d'indépendance. Je suivrai des cours qui m'intéressent; je ferai la connaissance de jeunes qui ont les mêmes intérêts et les mêmes goûts que moi.**

*(40 seconds)*

**(t) End of test.**

**Now look over your answers.**

*[END OF TRANSCRIPT]*

FOR OFFICIAL USE

C

Total Marks

# 1000/408

NATIONAL
QUALIFICATIONS
2003

WEDNESDAY, 14 MAY
2.30 PM – 3.00 PM
(APPROX)

FRENCH
STANDARD GRADE
Credit Level
Listening

**Fill in these boxes and read what is printed below.**

Full name of centre

Town

Forename(s)

Surname

Date of birth
Day Month Year

Scottish candidate number

Number of seat

When you are told to do so, open your paper.

You will hear a number of short items in French. You will hear each item three times, then you will have time to write your answer.

Write your answers, **in English**, in this book, in the appropriate spaces.

You may take notes as you are listening to the French, but only in this paper.

You may **not** use a French dictionary.

You are not allowed to leave the examination room until the end of the test.

Before leaving the examination room you must give this book to the invigilator. If you do not, you may lose all the marks for this paper.

SCOTTISH
QUALIFICATIONS
AUTHORITY

©

*Marks*

You hear a radio interview with Richard Giraud, a fifteen year old French boy who recently took part in an interesting, but unusual exchange.

Vous écoutez une interview avec Richard Giraud, un jeune Français de quinze ans, qui a récemment participé à un échange intéressant, mais pas vraiment typique.

1. Richard lives with his parents on a farm.

   What makes his lifestyle lonely? Mention any **two** things.

   2

   _____

   _____

   _____

   \*    \*    \*    \*    \*

2. What is his normal morning routine? Mention any **two** things.

   2

   _____

   _____

   _____

   \*    \*    \*    \*    \*

3. (*a*) What does he do when he gets home from school?

   1

   _____

   _____

   (*b*) Why does he go to bed early? Mention any **one** thing.

   1

   _____

   _____

   \*    \*    \*    \*    \*

*Marks*

**4.** (*a*) Why are Richard's parents sometimes concerned about him?     1

_____

_____

(*b*) Describe the exchange they organised for him.  Mention **two** things.     2

_____

_____

_____

\*     \*     \*     \*     \*

**5.** (*a*) What problem did Richard have at the beginning of the exchange?     1

_____

_____

(*b*) Why was this?  Mention any **one** thing.     1

_____

_____

\*     \*     \*     \*     \*

**6.** (*a*) What was he now able to do after school?  Mention any **two** things.     2

_____

_____

_____

(*b*) What information does he give about a school trip?  Mention **two** things.     2

_____

_____

_____

\*     \*     \*     \*     \*

**[Turn over for Questions 7 to 10 on *Page four***

*Marks*

**7.** During the exchange, Richard met his girlfriend, Véronique.

(*a*) Where did they meet?

1

_____

_____

(*b*) What does he say about Véronique? Mention any **two** things.

2

_____

_____

_____

\* \* \* \* \*

**8.** Véronique is hoping to go to university soon.

Why does she not enjoy school life? Mention **two** things.

2

_____

_____

_____

\* \* \* \* \*

**9.** What does she say about her part-time job? Mention any **two** things.

2

_____

_____

_____

\* \* \* \* \*

**10.** Véronique is looking forward to student life.

Why? Mention **three** things.

3

_____

_____

_____

_____

\* \* \* \* \*

**Total (25)**

*[END OF QUESTION PAPER]*

2004 | Credit

[BLANK PAGE]

C

Total

# 1000/403

NATIONAL
QUALIFICATIONS
2004

TUESDAY, 11 MAY
11.10 AM – 12.10 PM

FRENCH
STANDARD GRADE
Credit Level
Reading

**Fill in these boxes and read what is printed below.**

Full name of centre

Town

Forename(s)

Surname

Date of birth
Day  Month  Year

Scottish candidate number

Number of seat

When you are told to do so, open your paper and write your answers **in English** in the spaces provided.

You may use a French dictionary.

Before leaving the examination room you must give this book to the invigilator. If you do not, you may lose all the marks for this paper.

SCOTTISH
QUALIFICATIONS
AUTHORITY

©

DO NOT
WRITE I
THIS
MARGI

*Marks*

1. You read this article about the French police.

---

## Les policiers en ont assez!

D'habitude, les policiers vont aux manifestations pour surveiller les défilés, mais cette fois, ce sont *eux* qui ont manifesté les 10 et 17 novembre à Paris pour exprimer leur colère. Et pourquoi?

Eh bien, depuis le début de l'année, sept policiers ont été tués en France alors qu'ils exerçaient leur métier. Par exemple, au mois d'avril, deux agents essaient d'appréhender un cambrioleur dans le Val-de-Marne et sont assassinés. Et, au mois d'octobre, deux autres sont grièvement blessés quand ils arrêtent une voiture à Saint-Ouen, près de Paris. Au lieu de présenter ses papiers, l'automobiliste sort un pistolet et tire sur les agents.

---

(*a*)  What did French policemen do on 10th and 17th November?

1

_____

(*b*)  What happened in the incident in April? Mention **two** things.

2

_____

_____

(*c*)  Two policemen were seriously injured in Saint-Ouen in October. What happened? Mention **two** things.

2

_____

_____

_____

*Marks*

**2.** The article about the police continues.

"Ça suffit!" disent les policiers, et ils demandent une solution.

Le gouvernement a promis de recruter 3000 agents supplémentaires pour renforcer les troupes. En plus, on distribuera des gilets pare-balles pour protéger tous les agents qui travaillent dans la rue. Les hommes politiques savent bien que l'opinion publique est avec les forces de l'ordre!

(*a*) What has the government promised to do to help the police?
Mention **two** things.

2

_____

_____

(*b*) Why is the government taking this action?

1

_____

**[Turn over**

DO NO[T]
WRITE [IN]
THIS
MARGI[N]

*Marks*

**3.** You read this article about a possible new airport for Paris.

## Un aéroport de plus pour Paris?

Paris aura un troisième aéroport, après ceux d'Orly et de Roissy. Des sept sites possibles, c'est celui de Chaulnes, en Picardie, qui a été sélectionné. Selon les experts, cet endroit a le maximum d'avantages.

Situé à 125 kilomètres de Paris, il est relié à la capitale par l'autoroute et un Train à Grande Vitesse. Comme c'est une région peu peuplée, le survol des avions ne gênera pas trop de monde. C'est un avantage.

Mais le projet provoque beaucoup de crainte chez les habitants de la région. Ils estiment que le gouvernement a imposé son choix sans véritable discussion, et ils ne veulent pas subir le bruit et la pollution que le projet leur apportera.

(*a*) What transport links with Paris does the new site at Chaulnes, in Picardy, have?

2

_____

_____

(*b*) What other advantage does the area have? Mention any **one** thing.

1

_____

(*c*) Why are the local people opposed to the new airport?
Mention **two** things.

2

_____

_____

DO NOT
WRITE IN
THIS
MARGIN

*Marks*

**4.** The article about the new airport goes on.

> Et pourquoi, disent les habitants de la région, un nouvel aéroport, quand ceux de Roissy et d'Orly ne fonctionnent qu'à la moitié de leur capacité?
>
> Mais la construction de l'aéroport va prendre une dizaine d'années, et les experts disent que, entre-temps, le nombre de passagers va doubler – une augmentation que Roissy et Orly seront incapables d'absorber.

(*a*) Why do local people say the new airport is not required?

1

(*b*) How long will construction of the airport take?

1

(*c*) How is the new airport justified by the experts? Mention **two** things.

2

**[Turn over**

DO NO'
WRITE ▮
THIS
MARGI

*Marks*

**5.** You read this article about children who have to work.

## Les enfants travailleurs

### – des solutions difficiles.

Le 12 juin, l'Organisation Internationale du Travail (OIT) s'est réunie à Genève, en Suisse. Son but était d'alerter le monde au sujet des millions d'enfants qui travaillent. Ils sont 211 millions. Les plus nombreux vivent en Asie et dans le Pacifique.

Ces enfants doivent travailler pour aider leur famille. Sept sur dix sont employés dans des exploitations agricoles. Ils récoltent le tabac et le cacao.

(*a*) What was the purpose of the meeting held by OIT on 12th June?    1

_____

(*b*) Why are Asia and the Pacific countries mentioned?    1

_____

(*c*) Why do so many children have to work?    1

_____

(*d*) What do they do? Mention any **one** thing.    1

_____

*Marks*

**6.** The article about working children goes on.

Qui plus est, environ 10 millions sont employés dans les pays en voie de développement par les grandes entreprises internationales qui préfèrent engager des enfants puisque leurs salaires sont, bien sûr, moins élevés que ceux des adultes. Ces enfants fabriquent des habits, des chaussures, des tapis.

Grâce à des images chocs, qui ont fait le tour du monde, quelques entreprises ont voulu se présenter plus favorablement. Elles ont adopté un code de conduite, et elles n'emploient plus d'enfants. Mais le problème est difficile à régler. Si les enfants ne travaillent plus, que vont faire les familles qui dépendent de l'argent qu'ils gagnent? Ils risquent tous de mourir de faim.

*(a)* In which countries do many international companies employ children?     1

_____

*(b)* Why is this?     1

_____

*(c)* What do these children do?     1

_____

*(d)* What have these international companies now agreed to do?     1

_____

*(e)* Why might this not bring a solution to the problem?     1

_____

**Total (26)**

*[END OF QUESTION PAPER]*

[BLANK PAGE]

C

# 1000/409

<table>
<tr><td>NATIONAL<br>QUALIFICATIONS<br>2004</td><td>TUESDAY, 11 MAY<br>2.30 PM – 3.00 PM<br>(APPROX)</td><td>FRENCH<br>STANDARD GRADE<br>Credit Level<br>Listening Transcript</td></tr>
</table>

**This paper must not be seen by any candidate.**

The material overleaf is provided for use in an emergency only (eg the recording or equipment proving faulty) or where permission has been given in advance by SQA for the material to be read to candidates with special needs. The material must be read exactly as printed.

SCOTTISH
QUALIFICATIONS
AUTHORITY

**Transcript—Credit Level**

---

**Instructions to reader(s):**

For each item, read the English **once,** then read the French **three times**, with an interval of 5 seconds between the readings. On completion of the third reading, pause for the length of time indicated in brackets after each item, to allow the candidates to write their answers.

Where special arrangements have been agreed in advance to allow the reading of the material, those sections marked **(f)** should be read by a female speaker and those marked **(m)** by a male: those sections marked **(t)** should be read by the teacher.

---

**(t)** You are on holiday in France. You meet a young French girl called Nathalie.

**(m) or**
**(f)** **Tu passes des vacances en France. Tu fais la connaissance d'une jeune Française, Nathalie.**

**(t) Question number one.**

She tells you about her early life. What does she say? Mention any **two** things.

**(f)** **Moi, je suis née à Paris mais j'ai passé les sept premières années de ma vie en Algérie car mon père était diplomate.**

*(40 seconds)*

**(t) Question number two.**

She tells you about her family. What does she say? Mention any **one** thing.

**(f)** **Je suis la plus jeune de la famille. J'ai deux frères aînés. Ils sont plus âgés que moi de sept et neuf ans.**

*(40 seconds)*

**(t) Question number three.**

The family moved to Quebec in Canada. What difficulties did she experience there? Mention any **two** things.

**(f)** **En dix-neuf cent quatre-vingt-seize on a déménagé au Canada où on parle anglais et français. Au début, j'ai eu des difficultés à parler anglais et l'accent français était difficile à comprendre. En plus, ce n'était pas facile de se faire des amis.**

*(40 seconds)*

**(t) Question number four.**

She tells you what she liked best about her time in Canada. What did she like best about her time there? What does she say about where she went? Mention any **two** things.

**(f)** **Ce que j'aimais le plus, c'était les grandes vacances. Pendant un mois entier, on partait dans les vastes forêts; mon père louait une cabane au bord d'un lac à deux cents kilomètres de Québec.**

*(40 seconds)*

**(t) Question number five.**

She goes on to tell you more about this place. What does she say about it? Mention any **two** things.

**(f)**       **Dans le petit village près de la cabane, tout le monde se connaissait bien. Il y avait des jeunes de mon âge et j'ai vite perfectionné mon anglais.**

*(40 seconds)*

**(t) Question number six.**

She tells you about how she spent some of her free time in Canada. What does she say? Why did she have to give up this activity?

**(f)**       **Dans presque toutes les villes au Canada, il y a une patinoire et c'est là où j'ai appris à faire du patin à glace. Ça m'a vraiment passionnée. Malheureusement, à l'âge de treize ans, je me suis cassé la jambe et maintenant je ne peux plus patiner.**

*(40 seconds)*

**(t) Question number seven.**

Why does Nathalie not consider France her home? Which **two** family events does she refer to?

**(f)**       **Naturellement je suis française mais avant l'âge de seize ans, j'ai passé très peu de temps ici. Quand j'étais petite, j'ai visité la France seulement deux fois; une fois pour le mariage de mon cousin et puis il y a cinq ans quand mon grand-père est mort.**

*(40 seconds)*

**(t) Question number eight.**

She tells you about her family now. What information does she give? Mention any **two** things.

**(f)**       **Mes parents sont retournés en France il y a deux ans et mon père travaille dans un bureau dans la banlieue parisienne. Mes deux frères vivent toujours au Canada.**

*(40 seconds)*

**(t) Question number nine.**

What further information does Nathalie give about her family? Mention **two** things.

**(f)**       **Un de mes frères est marié avec trois enfants, et l'autre n'a pas d'emploi en ce moment; il est au chômage.**

*(40 seconds)*

**[Turn over for Questions 10 to 12 on *Page four***

**(t) Question number ten.**

One evening, you and Nathalie are listening to a radio phone-in programme. A French boy called Philippe asks a doctor for some advice.

What information does Philippe give about his eating habits? Mention **two** things. Why are his parents worried? Mention any **one** thing.

**(m)**      **Tous les jours, je mange à la cantine de mon collège et je vais deux ou trois fois par semaine au fastfood. Mes parents me disent que je risque d'avoir des problèmes de santé à l'avenir, parce que je ne mange pas bien.**

*(40 seconds)*

**(t) Question number eleven.**

What does the doctor say about staying healthy? Mention any **one** thing.

**(m) or**
**(f)**      **Être en bonne santé n'est pas seulement une question de nourriture. Le corps humain fonctionne au maximum quand on mange bien et quand on fait régulièrement de l'exercice physique.**

*(40 seconds)*

**(t) Question number twelve.**

What does the doctor recommend in order to stay fit? Mention any **two** things.

**(m) or**
**(f)**      **Alors, comment rester en forme? D'abord, aller à l'école à pied au lieu d'y aller en voiture avec papa. Et puis, aller au gymnase pour faire de l'exercice physique est moins pénible si tu le fais en groupe, avec des copains par exemple. Finalement, quand tu dois faire des courses pour ta mère, pourquoi pas y aller en vélo?**

*(40 seconds)*

**(t) End of test.**

**Now look over your answers.**

*[END OF TRANSCRIPT]*

FOR OFFICIAL USE

C

Total Marks

# 1000/408

NATIONAL
QUALIFICATIONS
2004

TUESDAY, 11 MAY
2.30 PM – 3.00 PM
(APPROX)

FRENCH
STANDARD GRADE
Credit Level
Listening

**Fill in these boxes and read what is printed below.**

Full name of centre

Town

Forename(s)

Surname

Date of birth

Day  Month  Year          Scottish candidate number          Number of seat

When you are told to do so, open your paper.

You will hear a number of short items in French. You will hear each item three times, then you will have time to write your answer.

Write your answers, **in English**, in this book, in the appropriate spaces.

You may take notes as you are listening to the French, but only in this paper.

You may **not** use a French dictionary.

You are not allowed to leave the examination room until the end of the test.

Before leaving the examination room you must give this book to the invigilator. If you do not, you may lose all the marks for this paper.

SCOTTISH
QUALIFICATIONS
AUTHORITY

*Marks*

You are on holiday in France.  You meet a young French girl called Nathalie.

Tu passes des vacances en France.  Tu fais la connaissance d'une jeune Française, Nathalie.

1.  She tells you about her early life.  What does she say?  Mention any **two** things.

    2

    _____

    _____

    \*       \*       \*       \*       \*

2.  She tells you about her family.  What does she say?  Mention any **one** thing.

    1

    _____

    _____

    \*       \*       \*       \*       \*

3.  The family moved to Quebec in Canada.  What difficulties did she experience there?  Mention any **two** things.

    2

    _____

    _____

    \*       \*       \*       \*       \*

4.  She tells you what she liked best about her time in Canada.

    (*a*)  What did she like best about her time there?

    1

    _____

    (*b*)  What does she say about where she went?  Mention any **two** things.

    2

    _____

    _____

    \*       \*       \*       \*       \*

*Marks*

**5.** She goes on to tell you more about this place.  What does she say about it?  Mention any **two** things.

2

_____

_____

\*    \*    \*    \*    \*

**6.** She tells you about how she spent some of her free time in Canada.

(*a*)    What does she say?

1

_____

(*b*)    Why did she have to give up this activity?

1

_____

_____

\*    \*    \*    \*    \*

**7.** (*a*)  Why does Nathalie not consider France her home?

1

_____

(*b*)  Which **two** family events does she refer to?

2

_____

_____

\*    \*    \*    \*    \*

**8.** She tells you about her family now.  What information does she give?  Mention any **two** things.

2

_____

_____

\*    \*    \*    \*    \*

**[Turn over for Questions 9 to 12 on *Page four***

*Marks*

9. What further information does Nathalie give about her family?  Mention **two** things.

2

_____

_____

\*     \*     \*     \*     \*

10. One evening, you and Nathalie are listening to a radio phone-in programme.  A French boy called Philippe asks a doctor for some advice.

    (*a*)  What information does Philippe give about his eating habits?  Mention **two** things.

2

_____

_____

    (*b*)  Why are his parents worried?  Mention any **one** thing.

1

_____

\*     \*     \*     \*     \*

11. What does the doctor say about staying healthy?  Mention any **one** thing.

1

_____

\*     \*     \*     \*     \*

12. What does the doctor recommend in order to stay fit?  Mention any **two** things.

2

_____

_____

\*     \*     \*     \*     \*

**Total (25)**

*[END OF QUESTION PAPER]*

2005 | Credit

**[BLANK PAGE]**

**C**

FOR OFFICIAL USE

| | | | | | |
|---|---|---|---|---|---|

Total

# 1000/403

NATIONAL
QUALIFICATIONS
2005

TUESDAY, 10 MAY
11.10 AM – 12.10 PM

FRENCH
STANDARD GRADE
Credit Level
Reading

---

**Fill in these boxes and read what is printed below.**

Full name of centre

Town

Forename(s)

Surname

Date of birth
Day  Month  Year

Scottish candidate number

Number of seat

When you are told to do so, open your paper and write your answers **in English** in the spaces provided.

You may use a French dictionary.

Before leaving the examination room you must give this book to the invigilator. If you do not, you may lose all the marks for this paper.

SCOTTISH
QUALIFICATIONS
AUTHORITY

©

You are reading a French magazine.

1.  You read an article about mobile phones.

### LES TÉLÉPHONES PORTABLES. . . JUSTE *POUR LA FRIME? VOICI QUELQUES OPINIONS.

Les téléphones portables, ça sert vraiment. Mes parents en ont un chacun et je peux les appeler n'importe quand - par exemple, si je suis malade au collège.

*Georges, 13 ans*

En classe de maths, un téléphone a sonné. Le prof était vraiment en colère et il l'a confisqué. Mais il y en avait encore une dizaine . . .

Je trouve que chez certains élèves, c'est un peu de la frime.

*Sarah, 15 ans*

Quand on lit un magazine dans le bus et qu'on les entend sonner, j'ai envie de les casser. Après tout, on se débrouillait sans problème avant les téléphones portables.

*Vanessa, 14 ans*

Les portables, c'est super! Depuis que j'en ai un, j'ai plus de liberté: le weekend, je peux aller en ville tout seul, et j'ai la permission de minuit. Dans quelques années, avoir un portable, ce sera aussi naturel que d'avoir un walkman.

*Pierre, 13 ans*

C'est une invention utile, je l'admets. Mais au collège, c'est complètement ridicule! Il y a certains élèves qui l'utilisent pour parler à un ami qui est à vingt mètres d'eux. Ça, c'est de la frime et ils me font rire!

*Jean-Luc, 15 ans*

*pour la frime = for show

*Marks*

**1. (continued)**

Complete the sentences.    5

Georges:  I can call my parents —————————————————————.

Sarah:    The maths teacher confiscated one but ——————————————

——————————————————————————————————————————.

Vanessa:  When phones ring on the bus I feel like ————————————.

Pierre:    At the weekend I can ——————————————————————.

Jean-Luc: Some pupils use them to speak to friends who ——————————

——————————————————————————————————————————.

**[Turn over**

DO NO
WRITE
THIS
MARG

*Marks*

**2.** You read an article about journalists.

### Journaliste: un métier à risque

Les journalistes ne sont pas toujours libres d'écrire et de dire ce qu'ils veulent. Parfois des journalistes sont tués, emprisonnés ou victimes de violence. Une organisation, *Reporters sans Frontières*, s'occupe de les défendre.

En 2003 il y a eu moins de journalistes tués qu'en 2002, vingt-cinq en tout. Par contre, les agressions et les violences ont été plus nombreuses, et il reste encore cent dix-huit journalistes emprisonnés. Selon un rapport de *Reporters sans Frontières*, la majorité des journalistes tués ont été assassinés par des groupes armés. Et des gouvernements aussi sont souvent responsables de la mort de certains journalistes.

(*a*) What restriction is sometimes placed on reporters?

1

_____

_____

(*b*) What facts are we told about incidents in 2003 regarding journalists? Mention any **two** things.

2

_____

_____

(*c*) Journalists are being killed all over the world. Which **two** groups are responsible for this?

2

_____

_____

DO NOT
WRITE IN
THIS
MARGIN

*Marks*

**3.** The article continues.

---

### Pour la liberté de la presse

Les journalistes sont aussi censurés: il leur est interdit d'écrire certaines choses qui pourraient gêner le gouvernement d'un pays par exemple. Il y a plusieurs années, cette censure était surtout pratiquée en Chine, en Turquie, en Iran et en Arabie Saoudite.

*Reporters sans Frontières* a besoin d'argent pour défendre les journalistes en prison et pour aider les familles de ceux qui sont morts ou qui ont dû fuir leur pays. Donc trois journalistes très connus en France ont décidé de vendre, dans les magasins de journaux, une collection de leurs photographies: "Pour la liberté de la presse". C'est une campagne "choc" pour la défense de la liberté de la presse.

---

(*a*) Journalists are often banned from writing about certain things in countries like China, Turkey, etc. Why is this?

1

_____

(*b*) The organisation "Reporters sans Frontières" is always trying to raise money. Why? Mention **three** things.

3

_____

_____

_____

(*c*) Three well known French journalists have agreed to help. What have they decided to do?

1

_____

**[Turn over**

*Marks*

**4.** You come across this article about Robbie Williams.

---

## Robbie Williams . . . une drôle de vie!

Robert Peter Williams est né le 13 février 1974 à Newcastle. Ses parents ont divorcé quand Robbie avait trois ans et après, il a vécu avec sa mère, Theresa. Il a aussi une soeur aînée, Sally.

C'est un neveu de sa soeur qui a trouvé pour Robbie son premier emploi: vendeur de fenêtres à double vitrage.

Les premières années de sa vie, il habitait une maison tout près d'un stade où s'entraînait Port Vale FC, son équipe préférée. A l'école, il était plutôt bon élève; il avait toujours de bonnes notes dans la plupart des matières.

Comme son père, Robbie se destinait à la comédie, mais à l'âge de 16 ans, il a été engagé pour former le groupe Take That. Après avoir quitté le groupe très fâché contre le producteur, il s'est lancé dans une carrière solo qui a mis plusieurs années à démarrer. Voilà pourquoi il a sombré dans l'alcool et la drogue.

Libéré de ses démons, Robbie a signé avec sa maison de disques un énorme contrat qui l'abritera du besoin d'argent jusqu' à la fin de ses jours.

---

(a) What was Robbie's first job and how did he get it?　　2

_____

_____

(b) How did he become a fan of Port Vale FC?　　1

_____

(c) What are we told about his schooldays? Mention **one** thing.　　1

_____

(d) According to the article, why did he have problems with alcohol and drugs?　　1

_____

(e) What will be the outcome of his new recording contract?　　1

_____

*Marks*

**5.** The article on Robbie Williams continues with an interview.

---

### Robbie: "J'adore venir en France . . ."

. . . interviewé par Claire Richard.

C.R. Tu as acheté une maison à Los Angeles et tu passes pas mal de temps en Californie. Alors, tu déménages aux Etats-Unis?

R.W. Non, je passe du temps dans le monde entier. Je voyage de pays en pays pour faire des concerts.

C.R. Tu vas bientôt donner deux concerts à Paris. Comment seront-ils, ces concerts?

R.W. Je ne sais pas exactement encore, mais il y aura des feux d'artifice. Ce seront, sans doute, des spectacles inoubliables!

C.R. Oui, tu commences à être bien apprécié en France. Il ne reste pas de billets pour les concerts.

R.W. C'est vrai, mais je ne sais pas si les Français me connaissent si bien que ça. Quand je fais des concerts en France ce sont les Britanniques qui achètent la plupart des billets. Quand même, j'adore venir en France. Les gens sont très sympas.

C.R. Et le côté romantique?

R.W. Dans le passé, j'ai eu beaucoup de petites copines et j'en aurai encore. Je trouve difficile de résister à une belle fille.

---

(a) Why does the interviewer think Robbie is moving to the USA? Mention any **one** thing.

1

_____

(b) What will his concerts in Paris be like? Mention **one** thing.

1

_____

(c) According to Robbie, why are his French concerts so well-attended?

1

_____

(d) What does Robbie say about girls? Mention any **two** things.

2

_____

_____

*[END OF QUESTION PAPER]*

**Total (26)**

[BLANK PAGE]

C

# 1000/409

| | | |
|---|---|---|
| NATIONAL QUALIFICATIONS 2005 | TUESDAY, 10 MAY 2.30 PM – 3.00 PM (APPROX) | **FRENCH STANDARD GRADE** Credit Level Listening Transcript |

**This paper must not be seen by any candidate.**

The material overleaf is provided for use in an emergency only (eg the recording or equipment proving faulty) or where permission has been given in advance by SQA for the material to be read to candidates with special needs. The material must be read exactly as printed.

SCOTTISH
QUALIFICATIONS
AUTHORITY

### Transcript—Credit Level

**Instructions to reader(s):**

For each item, read the English **once,** then read the French **three times**, with an interval of 5 seconds between the readings. On completion of the third reading, pause for the length of time indicated in brackets after each item, to allow the candidates to write their answers.

Where special arrangements have been agreed in advance to allow the reading of the material, those sections marked **(f)** should be read by a female speaker and those marked **(m)** by a male: those sections marked **(t)** should be read by the teacher.

**(t)** You are taking part in an exchange visit to France. When you arrive at your pen friend Marc's house, you learn that he is in hospital and you go to visit him.

**(m)**
or
**(f)**
**Tu participes à un échange scolaire en France. Quand tu arrives chez ton correspondant Marc, tu apprends qu'il est à l'hôpital et tu vas le voir.**

**(t) Question number one.**

Marc tells you about the events leading up to him being in hospital. What does he say? Mention **two** things.

**(m)**
**Samedi dernier c'était la Fête de la Musique dans le village. L'après-midi il y avait au moins douze orchestres et beaucoup de danseurs dans la rue principale.**

*(40 seconds)*

**(t) Question number two.**

He goes on to explain what happened to him. What does he say? Mention any **two** things.

**(m)**
**Dans la rue il y avait énormément de spectateurs. On m'a poussé par derrière et je suis tombé. J'ai su immédiatement que c'était grave. Et, ici, à l'hôpital, ils ont diagnostiqué une jambe cassée.**

*(40 seconds)*

**(t) Question number three.**

He tells you about his stay in hospital. Why was he not happy at first? Why is he happier now?

**(m)**
**Au début, j'étais dans une salle avec beaucoup de personnes âgées, mais maintenant ça va mieux parce que je suis dans une chambre avec trois personnes de mon âge.**

*(40 seconds)*

**(t) Question number four.**

He tells you about the food in the hospital. What does he say? Mention any **two** things.

**(m)**
**Les repas ne sont pas aussi bons que chez moi. Parfois il y a des plats que je n'aime pas du tout. Alors, je téléphone à ma mère et elle m'apporte quelque chose à manger.**

*(40 seconds)*

**(t) Question number five.**

When will Marc get home from hospital? What does he suggest you do till then?

**(m)** **Je dois rester à l'hôpital jusqu'à la fin de la semaine. Donc, je propose que tu passes ces quatre jours chez mon ami, Gérard, qui habite pas loin d'ici.**

*(40 seconds)*

**(t) Question number six.**

When you arrive at Gérard's house, his mother speaks to you. How long have Marc and Gérard known each other? How did they get to know each other? Mention any **two** things.

**(f)** **Marc et Gérard se connaissent depuis onze ans. A ce moment-là, nos deux familles habitaient la même rue. Les deux garçons avaient le même âge, donc ils étaient dans la même classe à l'école primaire.**

*(40 seconds)*

**(t) Question number seven.**

You are introduced to Gérard, who tells you what he and Marc used to do every day. What did they do? Mention any **two** things. What happened in the evenings?

**(m)** **On se voyait tous les jours. Le matin, on allait à l'école à vélo; à midi, on mangeait à la cantine, et on rentrait ensemble à la fin de la journée. Après le repas du soir, ou bien Marc venait chez moi, ou bien j'allais chez lui pour jouer.**

*(40 seconds)*

**(t) Question number eight.**

What did the boys do on holiday last year? Mention any **two** things. What was Gérard particularly pleased about?

**(m)** **L'année dernière, nous sommes partis en vacances ensemble. Nous avons passé un mois à la montagne. On a fait beaucoup d'activités—des randonnées à cheval, de l'escalade et du ski nautique. Ce qui m'a vraiment plu, c'est qu'on a fait la connaissance de beaucoup de jeunes de tous les coins de la France.**

*(40 seconds)*

**(t) Question number nine.**

Gérard goes on to talk about the future. Complete the sentences.

**(m)** **Marc et moi, nous allons peut-être nous retrouver à l'université. Comme tu le sais déjà, Marc est fort en langues vivantes; et moi, je voudrais devenir pharmacien. De toute façon, je suis sûr que j'ai trouvé un ami pour toute la vie.**

*(40 seconds)*

**[Turn over for Question 10 on *Page four***

**(t) Question number ten.**

According to Gérard's mother, how will life at home change when Gérard goes to university? Mention any **one** thing. What do Gérard's parents complain about at the moment? Mention any **two** things.

**(f)**     **Quand Gérard partira pour l'université, la vie chez nous sera beaucoup plus tranquille. En ce moment, il y a souvent des disputes à la maison. Son père et moi, on trouve que Gérard rentre trop tard à la maison pendant la semaine; il laisse toujours sa chambre en désordre, et puis, il passe trop de temps devant la télévision.**

*( 40 seconds )*

**(t) End of test.**

**Now look over your answers.**

*[END OF TRANSCRIPT]*

C

Total Marks

# 1000/408

NATIONAL QUALIFICATIONS 2005

TUESDAY, 10 MAY 2.30 PM – 3.00 PM (APPROX)

FRENCH STANDARD GRADE
Credit Level
Listening

**Fill in these boxes and read what is printed below.**

Full name of centre

Town

Forename(s)

Surname

Date of birth
Day Month Year     Scottish candidate number     Number of seat

When you are told to do so, open your paper.

You will hear a number of short items in French. You will hear each item three times, then you will have time to write your answer.

Write your answers, **in English**, in this book, in the appropriate spaces.

You may take notes as you are listening to the French, but only in this paper.

You may **not** use a French dictionary.

You are not allowed to leave the examination room until the end of the test.

Before leaving the examination room you must give this book to the invigilator. If you do not, you may lose all the marks for this paper.

SCOTTISH QUALIFICATIONS AUTHORITY

THB 1000/408 6/22470

©

DO NO
WRITE
THIS
MARG

*Marks*

You are taking part in an exchange visit to France. When you arrive at your pen friend Marc's house, you learn that he is in hospital and you go to visit him.

Tu participes à un échange scolaire en France. Quand tu arrives chez ton correspondant Marc, tu apprends qu'il est à l'hôpital et tu vas le voir.

1. Marc tells you about the events leading up to him being in hospital. What does he say? Mention **two** things.

2

_____

_____

\*　　\*　　\*　　\*　　\*

2. He goes on to explain what happened to him. What does he say? Mention any **two** things.

2

_____

_____

\*　　\*　　\*　　\*　　\*

3. He tells you about his stay in hospital.

   (*a*) Why was he not happy at first?

1

_____

   (*b*) Why is he happier now?

1

_____

\*　　\*　　\*　　\*　　\*

4. He tells you about the food in the hospital. What does he say? Mention any **two** things.

2

_____

_____

\*　　\*　　\*　　\*　　\*

Marks

**5.** (*a*)  When will Marc get home from hospital?

_____    1

(*b*)  What does he suggest you do till then?

_____    1

_____

\*      \*      \*      \*      \*

**6.** When you arrive at Gérard's house, his mother speaks to you.

(*a*)  How long have Marc and Gérard known each other?    1

_____

(*b*)  How did they get to know each other?  Mention any **two** things.    2

_____

_____

\*      \*      \*      \*      \*

**7.** You are introduced to Gérard, who tells you what he and Marc used to do every day.

(*a*)  What did they do?  Mention any **two** things.    2

_____

_____

(*b*)  What happened in the evenings?    1

_____

\*      \*      \*      \*      \*

**[Turn over for Questions 8 to 10 on *Page four***

*Marks*

**8.** (*a*)   What did the boys do on holiday last year?  Mention any **two** things.

2

_____

_____

(*b*)   What was Gérard particularly pleased about?

1

_____

\*     \*     \*     \*     \*

**9.**   Gérard goes on to talk about the future.  Complete the sentences.

3

Both boys hope to go to university.

Marc is good at _____.

Gérard wants to be _____.

Gérard is sure that he has found _____.

\*     \*     \*     \*     \*

**10.** (*a*)   According to Gérard's mother, how will life at home change when Gérard goes to university?  Mention any **one** thing.

1

_____

(*b*)   What do Gérard's parents complain about at the moment?  Mention any **two** things.

2

_____

_____

\*     \*     \*     \*     \*

**Total (25)**

[*END OF QUESTION PAPER*]

**2006** | Credit

[BLANK PAGE]

FOR OFFICIAL USE

C

Total

## 1000/403

NATIONAL
QUALIFICATIONS
2006

TUESDAY, 9 MAY
11.10 AM – 12.10 PM

**FRENCH
STANDARD GRADE**
Credit Level
Reading

**Fill in these boxes and read what is printed below.**

Full name of centre

Town

Forename(s)

Surname

Date of birth
Day Month Year      Scottish candidate number      Number of seat

When you are told to do so, open your paper and write your answers **in English** in the spaces provided.

You may use a French dictionary.

Before leaving the examination room you must give this book to the invigilator. If you do not, you may lose all the marks for this paper.

SCOTTISH
QUALIFICATIONS
AUTHORITY

©

DO NO
WRITE
THI
MARG

*Marks*

You are reading a French magazine.

1. A girl has written to the advice page of the magazine with some concerns about smoking.

> **Chère Anne!**
>
> Beaucoup de mes amies fument déjà, et elles n'arrêtent pas de me dire que fumer c'est extra, et que je devrais essayer.
>
> J'ai peur qu'elles ne me parlent plus si je refuse de fumer avec elles.  Que dois-je faire?
>
> *Bernadette, 13 ans.*

Complete the sentences.

(*a*) Bernadette's friends say that smoking is _____    **2**

and that she _____ .

(*b*) If Bernadette refuses, she is afraid that her friends _____    **1**

_____ .

*Marks*

**2.** The editor of the magazine has answered Bernadette's letter.

---

Fumer ou ne pas fumer, c'est une décision pour chaque individu.

Il faut savoir que . . .

. . . presque la moitié des jeunes Français âgés de 15 à 24 ans fument.

. . . les filles qui fument sont de plus en plus nombreuses et elles sont plus jeunes quand elles commencent à fumer.

Dans quelques années, tes copines auront la mauvaise haleine et les doigts jaunes – sans parler de maladies bien plus graves.  En expliquant tout ça à tes copines, tu peux leur montrer que tu as de très bonnes raisons pour dire "non" à la cigarette.

Tu sais que, depuis le début de l'année, les médias refusent de donner une image positive des fumeurs.  Au contraire ils informent le public des dangers du tabac pour la santé.

---

(*a*)  What statistic is given about French people between the ages of 15 and 24?    1

_____

(*b*)  What information is given about girls?  Mention any **one** thing.    1

_____

_____

(*c*)  What problems will Bernadette's friends have in a few years?  Mention any **two** things.    2

_____

_____

(*d*)  How are the media helping in the campaign against smoking?  Mention any **one** thing.    1

_____

**[Turn over**

*Marks*

3.    You come across an article about an environmental problem.

---

### La France sous les déchets

Vous avez vu tous les emballages qu'on jette à la poubelle quand on revient du supermarché?  La société est devenue trop gourmande en emballage. En 1975 un Français produisait 500g d'ordures ménagères par jour. Aujourd'hui il en produit un kilo.

Le Ministre de l'Ecologie lance un plan d'action.  Elle demande aux consommateurs de faire des efforts pour utiliser moins d'emballages. Comme ça on va gaspiller moins de papier.

Une grande campagne de publicité va encourager les Français à acheter des produits qui respectent l'environnement et à réutiliser les sacs plastiques.

---

(*a*)  What has doubled since 1975?                                          **1**

_____

_____

(*b*)  (i)   What does the Minister for the Environment want people to do?    **2**

_____

(ii)  Why?

_____

(*c*)  What is the purpose of the publicity campaign?  Mention **two** things.    **2**

_____

_____

*Marks*

**4.** You read an article about the work of a pharmacist.

---

*Marcel, 52 ans, pharmacien dans un village du Haut-Rhin.*

Je voulais faire quelque chose dans le domaine des sciences et au lycée j'aimais la biochimie et la physique, donc j'ai étudié la pharmacologie à l'université.

Les pharmaciens ont six ans d'étude après le bac, donc ils finissent leurs études assez tard, à l'âge de 23 ans ou plus. Deux pharmaciens sur trois travaillent dans les pharmacies et les autres dans les laboratoires des hôpitaux et chez les fabricants de médicaments.

Pour faire ce métier, il faut s'intéresser aux gens et s'entendre bien avec ses clients. Mes clients me racontent leurs problèmes de santé et je leur explique les ordonnances.

---

(a) Why did Marcel choose to study pharmacy? Mention any **one** thing.　　1

_____

_____

(b) What does he say about becoming a pharmacist? Mention any **one** thing.　　1

_____

_____

(c) Apart from pharmacies, where do most pharmacists work? Mention **two** things.　　2

_____

_____

(d) What does he say about his job? Mention any **two** things.　　2

_____

_____

**[Turn over**

Marks

**5.** You read an article in which young French people discuss whether machines are good or bad for society.

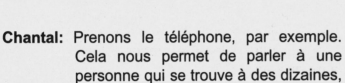

**Les machines nous apportent des biens. Oui! Mais ......**

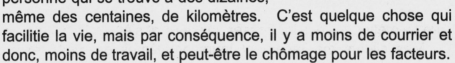

**Chantal:** Prenons le téléphone, par exemple. Cela nous permet de parler à une personne qui se trouve à des dizaines, même des centaines, de kilomètres. C'est quelque chose qui facilitie la vie, mais par conséquence, il y a moins de courrier et donc, moins de travail, et peut-être le chômage pour les facteurs.

**Mathieu:** Plus on a de machines, plus on a de besoins. Par exemple, on a inventé le portable. Mais, pour les faire fonctionner, on a besoin de chargeurs et d'un réseau.

**Thierry:** Et maintenant il y a les ordinateurs. Dans l'avenir, les ordinateurs feront tout le travail des hommes, mais les gens ne vont pas s'ennuyer. Au lieu de travailler, ils pourront consacrer tout leur temps à s'amuser.

(*a*) According to Chantal the telephone has been a useful invention. But, what are the disadvantages? Mention any **two** things.

2

_____

_____

(*b*) What invention does Mathieu talk about?

1

_____

(*c*) Why is it of little use on its own?

1

_____

(*d*) What does Thierry say about the effect of computers? Mention **three** things.

3

_____

_____

*[END OF QUESTION PAPER]*

**Total (26)**

**[BLANK PAGE]**

[BLANK PAGE]

**C**

# 1000/409

NATIONAL
QUALIFICATIONS
2006

TUESDAY, 9 MAY
2.30 PM – 3.00 PM
(APPROX)

FRENCH
STANDARD GRADE
Credit Level
Listening Transcript

**This paper must not be seen by any candidate.**

The material overleaf is provided for use in an emergency only (eg the recording or equipment proving faulty) or where permission has been given in advance by SQA for the material to be read to candidates with additional support needs. The material must be read exactly as printed.

SCOTTISH
QUALIFICATIONS
AUTHORITY

©

**Transcript—Credit Level**

---

**Instructions to reader(s):**

For each item, read the English **once,** then read the French **three times**, with an interval of 5 seconds between the readings. On completion of the third reading, pause for the length of time indicated in brackets after each item, to allow the candidates to write their answers.

Where special arrangements have been agreed in advance to allow the reading of the material, those sections marked **(f)** should be read by a female speaker and those marked **(m)** by a male: those sections marked **(t)** should be read by the teacher.

---

**(t)** You are spending your holidays with your family in a hotel in France.

**(m) or (f)**  **Tu passes les vacances avec ta famille dans un hôtel en France.**

**(t) Question number one.**

You meet a French boy called Georges who introduces you to his twin sister, Nicole. What does he say?

**(m)**  **Voici ma soeur, Nicole. Nous sommes jumeaux. Heureusement, nous nous entendons très bien. J'ai de très bons rapports avec elle.**

*(40 seconds)*

**(t) Question number two.**

Georges' mother tells you about their holidays. What does she say? Mention any **two** things.

**(f)**  **En général, on passe seulement une semaine ici en juillet parce que mon mari doit travailler. Pour nous, les vacances principales sont en hiver. Nous passons une quinzaine à faire du ski en Suisse.**

*(40 seconds)*

**(t) Question number three.**

She then explains what there is to do in the area. What does she say? Mention any **two** things.

**(f)**  **Passer les vacances ici, ça me plaît beaucoup. Il y a tant de choses à faire pour les jeunes. Il y a un parc d'attractions pas loin d'ici. Et en plus, on peut faire de l'équitation.**

*(40 seconds)*

**(t) Question number four.**

Georges talks about his sporting activities. What does he tell you? Mention any **two** things.

**(m)**  **Moi, j'ai la chance d'être doué pour le sport. Je fais des sports d'équipe et des sports individuels. Au collège, je suis champion de natation.**

*(40 seconds)*

**(t) Question number five.**

What did he do during the Easter holidays? Mention any **two** things.

**(m)**     Pendant les vacances de Pâques, j'ai travaillé dans un club pour les enfants âgés de cinq à dix ans. C'était une expérience formidable pour moi! J'ai passé toute la journée en plein air avec les enfants.

*(40 seconds)*

**(t) Question number six.**

What does Georges say about his school subjects? What does he say about the kind of job he wants? Mention any **one** thing.

**(m)**     Je ne suis pas fort en maths et en français. Être assis dans un bureau ne m'intéresse pas du tout. Je sais que je dois trouver un métier où je serai tout le temps actif.

*(40 seconds)*

**(t) Question number seven.**

Nicole tells you she wants to be a librarian. What does she say about her childhood which shows her interest in books? Mention **two** things.

**(f)**     Depuis très longtemps, je veux devenir bibliothécaire. Quand j'étais enfant, je lisais avec enthousiasme des livres de toutes sortes. Quelquefois, j'oubliais de venir manger avec la famille parce que je voulais finir mon livre.

*(40 seconds)*

**(t) Question number eight.**

What has Nicole done to prepare herself for the job of librarian? Mention **two** things.

**(f)**     Au mois de juillet, j'ai travaillé dans la bibliothèque municipale de notre ville. J'ai remplacé un bibliothécaire qui était en vacances. C'était intéressant et très utile pour moi.

*(40 seconds)*

**(t) Question number nine.**

Libraries are not just for lending books. For what other reasons do people go there? Mention **two** things.

**(f)**     Tu sais, aujourd'hui, le travail de bibliothécaire ne consiste pas seulement à distribuer les livres. Dans presque toutes les bibliothèques, on trouve des ordinateurs et beaucoup de gens viennent chercher des informations sur Internet. Et il y a aussi des étudiants qui doivent faire des recherches pour préparer leurs examens.

*(40 seconds)*

**[Turn over for Questions 10 to 13 on *Page four***

**(t) Question number ten.**

Their father talks about his first job helping his uncle. What did his uncle do for a living? How did he help him?

**(m)**      **Mon oncle avait une petite ferme où il cultivait des fruits et des légumes. A l'âge de quinze ans, je l'aidais à transporter les produits au marché tous les samedi matins.**

*(40 seconds)*

**(t) Question number eleven.**

What does Nicole say about her mother? She sometimes has problems with her dad. Why? Mention any **one** thing.

**(f)**      **Dans l'ensemble, ma mère me traite comme une adulte mais quelquefois j'ai des problèmes avec mon père. Il est protecteur quand je veux sortir. Il ne comprend pas que je ne suis plus une enfant.**

*(40 seconds)*

**(t) Question number twelve.**

Their mother also talks about what happens when young people go to university. What does she say? Mention any **two** things.

**(f)**      **Quand les jeunes vont à l'université ils veulent être indépendants, bien sûr! Mais ils sont souvent influencés par les autres et il y a toujours la tentation de prendre de la drogue ou de trop boire.**

*(40 seconds)*

**(t) Question number thirteen.**

What does their father say about Nicole and Georges and the work they will do? Mention any **two** things.

**(m)**      **Nicole et Georges, ils sont très différents l'un de l'autre. Mais ce qu'ils feront dans la vie ne m'inquiète pas. L'important, c'est qu'ils trouvent un métier où ils sont heureux, un emploi qui leur plaît.**

*(40 seconds)*

**(t) End of test.**

**Now look over your answers.**

*[END OF TRANSCRIPT]*

FOR OFFICIAL USE

C

Total Marks

# 1000/408

NATIONAL
QUALIFICATIONS
2006

TUESDAY, 9 MAY
2.30 PM – 3.00 PM
(APPROX)

## FRENCH
## STANDARD GRADE
Credit Level
Listening

**Fill in these boxes and read what is printed below.**

Full name of centre

Town

Forename(s)

Surname

Date of birth
Day Month Year

Scottish candidate number

Number of seat

When you are told to do so, open your paper.

You will hear a number of short items in French. You will hear each item three times, then you will have time to write your answer.

Write your answers, **in English**, in this book, in the appropriate spaces.

You may take notes as you are listening to the French, but only in this paper.

You may **not** use a French dictionary.

You are not allowed to leave the examination room until the end of the test.

Before leaving the examination room you must give this book to the invigilator. If you do not, you may lose all the marks for this paper.

SCOTTISH
QUALIFICATIONS
AUTHORITY

©

*Marks*

You are spending your holidays with your family in a hotel in France.

Tu passes les vacances avec ta famille dans un hôtel en France.

1. You meet a French boy called Georges who introduces you to his twin sister, Nicole. What does he say?

                1

_____

_____

\*     \*     \*     \*     \*

2. Georges' mother tells you about their holidays. What does she say? Mention any **two** things.

                2

_____

_____

\*     \*     \*     \*     \*

3. She then explains what there is to do in the area. What does she say? Mention any **two** things.

                2

_____

_____

\*     \*     \*     \*     \*

4. Georges talks about his sporting activities. What does he tell you? Mention any **two** things.

                2

_____

_____

\*     \*     \*     \*     \*

*Marks*

**5.** What did he do during the Easter holidays? Mention any **two** things.

_____

_____

2

\*     \*     \*     \*     \*

**6.** (*a*) What does Georges say about his school subjects?

_____

_____

1

(*b*) What does he say about the kind of job he wants? Mention any **one** thing.

_____

_____

1

\*     \*     \*     \*     \*

**7.** Nicole tells you she wants to be a librarian. What does she say about her childhood which shows her interest in books? Mention **two** things.

_____

_____

2

\*     \*     \*     \*     \*

**8.** What has Nicole done to prepare herself for the job of librarian? Mention **two** things.

_____

_____

2

\*     \*     \*     \*     \*

**[Turn over**

*Marks*

**9.** Libraries are not just for lending books. For what other reasons do people go there? Mention **two** things.

2

_____

_____

\*        \*        \*        \*        \*

**10.** Their father talks about his first job helping his uncle.

(*a*)    What did his uncle do for a living?

1

_____

(*b*)    How did he help him?

1

_____

\*        \*        \*        \*        \*

**11.** (*a*)    What does Nicole say about her mother?

1

_____

(*b*)    She sometimes has problems with her dad. Why? Mention any **one** thing.

1

_____

\*        \*        \*        \*        \*

**12.** Their mother also talks about what happens when young people go to university. What does she say? Mention any **two** things.

2

_____

_____

\*        \*        \*        \*        \*

*Marks*

**13.** What does their father say about Nicole and Georges and the work they will do?  Mention any **two** things.

2

_____

_____

\*        \*        \*        \*        \*

**Total (25)**

*[END OF QUESTION PAPER]*

[BLANK PAGE]

**[BLANK PAGE]**

[BLANK PAGE]

**[BLANK PAGE]**

Official SQA Past Papers: Credit French 2006

# Pocket answer section for
# SQA Credit French
# 2002–2006

© 2006 Scottish Qualifications Authority, All Rights Reserved
Published by Leckie & Leckie Ltd, 3rd Floor, 4 Queen Street, Edinburgh EH2 1JE
tel: 0131 220 6831, fax: 0131 225 9987, enquiries@leckieandleckie.co.uk, www.leckieandleckie.co.uk

## French Credit Level
## Reading 2002

1. (a) • it's our world/planet
we're all on the same planet/
because everyone lives in the world
   • we have to protect/defend it/
there's no-one else to protect it/
if we don't protect it no-one else will
   **(1 from 2)**

   (b) • put rubbish/waste/litter/
refuse/trash/garbage in the bin/
don't drop litter
   • towns/the place would be cleaner/
to clean up towns/the place

   (c) • respect the/their/your environment (better)

2. (a) • watch/check/monitor/keep an eye on
pedestrians/people <u>in the street</u>(s)
   • (police could) fine people for
dropping paper(s)/cigarette
end(s)/rubbish

   (b) • people/countries should forget their
differences (to find a solution)
   • everything/everywhere/the world/
the earth will be destroyed/
we'll risk being destroyed

3. (a) • if 2 people love each other, it'll last a
<u>lifetime</u> (without marriage)
   • don't need a contract
contract is just a piece of paper
   • contract not always/sometimes not
respected
   • lots of/increasing number of divorces
   • people (can) live (together) <u>happily/
successfully</u> without being married
   **(2 from 5)**

   (b) • to have a family/children
   • it's a legal bond/link/connection/for
legal reasons
   • social recognition/acceptance
   • important/better for children/
it helps the children/
it's in the children's (best) interest
   **(3 from 4)**

4. (a) • show God/friends they've found/
chosen/picked the right/a good partner
   • it's <u>only/just</u> a ritual/tradition/
it has no meaning

4. (b) • it's the start of a new/different life/
it's a new beginning
   • it's an unforgettable day
   • the (beautiful/white/wedding) dress

   **or** the celebration/feast/reception party
   **or** the presents
   **(2 from 3)**

5. (a) • sad: dull/dark/sombre/solemn/sober/
uninteresting/sad colours/colours like
black/navy blue/beige/grey
   • happy/sadness gone:
multicoloured clothes/bright colours/
lots of colours
   • depressed: big sweaters/jumpers/
jerseys/pullovers
   • in a good mood/feeling good/on form:
smart/chic/trendy/elegant clothes
   **(2 from 4)**
   Example: He wears different colours/kinds
of clothes to show what mood he's in =
1 point.

   (b) • he spends half his money/budget/
allowance/cash/pocket-money on clothes

6. • wears comfortable clothes/clothes she
feels relaxed in
   • wears what she likes/what pleases her
   • if it's not the latest fashion, doesn't
matter/not important
   • if friends don't like it, doesn't matter/
not important
   • prefers <u>spending money</u> on other/
things/more important things/going
out/video/computer games/music
   **(3 from 5)**

7. • easy to wash/clean
   • can wear different things with them/
they're easy to match/go with anything/
can wear elegant shirt/blouse or t-shirt
with them/
can wear something smart **or**
something casual
   • doesn't get ridiculed/laughed at/teased
   • doesn't want to be different (from
friends)/
wants to be like friends
   **(3 from 4)**

# French Credit Level
# Listening 2002

1. • works with wood/he's a joiner/
carpenter
   • makes/fabricates tables/furniture
   **(1 from 2)**

2. • <u>on a boat</u> between England and
France/going to/coming from
France/England/<u>on a boat</u> in the
Channel

3. • he/they lived there for 3 months
   • parents did a house exchange (with
friends)/stayed at a friend's house
   • sister went to school
   • he was too young to go to school
   **(3 from 4)**

4. • doesn't like snack lunches/lunch in Scotland/
in Scotland lunch is a snack/fast-food/
in Scotland lunch is often a sandwich,
crisps and a (fizzy) drink
(2 specifics required)
   • in France they eat a big/bigger/
proper meal at lunch time/12

   **NB Do not insist on use of lunch (time).
   If meal mentioned it must be lunch
   or dinner.**

5. • most people find the climate in Scotland
hard/harsh/awful/
most people do not like the Scottish weather
   • he doesn't mind the Scottish weather/
it doesn't bother him
   • he likes/loves/rain/wind
   **(2 from 3)**
   eg most people don't like the Scottish weather
   but he does = 1 point

6. • they liked/preferred the (French) way of life
   • life/it was more simple/simpler
   • they liked/preferred the freedom/liberty/they
had more freedom/for the freedom
   • life/it was less stressful/people are less
stressed/not a lot of stress in France/in
Scotland life was more stressful
   **(2 from 4)**

7. • they had lived in the same village for many/
15 years/a long time
   • parents/they needed a change/for a change
   • (they wanted) to travel (the world)/
see/go round the world/see new countries
   • to improve their/his/the children's English/to
(make) progress in English/to learn English
better
   **(3 from 4)**

8. (a) • save (up)/economise (for several years)
   • find a school/schools (for the children)
   **(1 from 2)**

   (b) • their friend found them a flat/house/
accommodation/
they had a flat arranged/waiting/
ready/organised for them/
they had a flat to go to

9. (a) • travelled/toured(around) (the country
for a month)

   (b) • Mum gave music lessons/taught music/
was a music teacher
   • Dad worked as a gardener/did gardening/
worked in a garden(s)

   **NB Mum and Dad are not essential
   but if used, jobs must match the
   person.**

10. • teachers listened to/were interested in (all)
pupils/you
   • teachers gave interesting/good lessons/
work/classes/courses/subjects were interesting
   • pupils had (more/lots of) freedom
   • school/lessons/classes started later/
school/lessons/classes finished earlier

   **NB There are fewer hours = 1 point.
   There are fewer hours and school
   started later = 1 point.**

11. • the <u>beauty</u> of nature/scenery/landscape/
countryside/country/place/environment/
its beauty/
natural beauty
   • they/the individual respect(s) the/their
<u>environment</u>/the <u>environment</u> is respected
   • it's/everything is clean/
very little/no litter/paper(s) (in the street/
roads) (lying about)/
the tidiness of the streets/roads
   **(2 from 3)**

## French Credit Level
## Reading 2003

1. • was **reduced/limited/cut/lowered** to 10 hours
   • a **compulsory/obligatory** day off/day of rest/ rest day/holiday
   • two weeks'/a fortnight **paid**/holiday/leave

2. (a) • **More than/over/upwards** of 3 million people are unemployed/don't work/are out of work/don't have a job
   • 700,000 (of them) are **under/less than** 25

   (b) To limit/restrict the (working) week **to 35 hours**/ To reduce the (working) week (from 39)/**by 4 hours**

   (c) They/(about) 70% of them would agree/be willing/be prepared to earn/agree to earning (a little) less **and** work less/have more leisure time/time off

   (d) **Some/certain** employers/bosses/managers/ leaders of enterprise(s)/business owners

   (e) A **meeting** of government, workers and employers/bosses/chiefs/companies to (try to) find a solution

3. (a) Any three from:
   • it gives/prints/decides on/tells/writes (a list of the) ingredients
   • it gives method (of cooking)/it tells/shows you how to cook/do it
   • it gives cooking time/it tells you how long to cook it for/time of cooking
   • it switches on/lights/starts/puts on the cooker
   • it controls/monitors the temperature of oven/cooker

   (b) send (electronic) message/e-mail to/contact **computer** (from car) hot plate

   (c) Any three from:
   • it/computer reads/registers/records/ remembers bar-code
   • (constantly) notes/keeps track of/monitors/ records the contents (of the fridge)
   • it sends an order to supermarket/tells the supermarket what you need
   • the firm/shop/supermarket/shopkeeper delivers/ sends it

4. (a) Any two from:
   • you order/ask for/request/programme/it/ it can be ordered by remote (control)/from anywhere/any room in house
   • programme/select/choose time/hour **and** temperature
   • bath fills automatically/itself

   (b) • wall becomes/turns into/is/will be/would be a (giant) screen
   • (loud) speakers in every corner of/in (four) corners of/(all) around the room

4. (c) **computer** will adjust/sort/set mattress to your position/shape/liking/to make you comfortable/to what you want

5. (a) to avoid bringing in/importing/introducing/ spreading disease/illness/ in case they're carrying disease(s)

   (b) • it will verify/check/confirm where/which country the animal/has come/it comes from/the animal's/its origin
   • its state of health/physical state/condition/ whether the animal's healthy

# French Credit Level
# Listening 2003

1. Any two from:
   - He's an only/single child/
     He has no brothers or sisters
   - They live/the farm is 22 kms from the town/the next town
   - It is/they are/the farm is (very) isolated/in the middle of nowhere
   - He/they rarely have visitors/receive visitors/people rarely visit/hardly anyone comes to visit/don't have/a lot of many visitors

2. Any two from:
   - Gets up at 5.45(am)
   - Helps father with the cows/cattle
   - Eats/has breakfast **quickly**
   - Gets bus/coach to **school/town**

3. (a) Homework

   (b) Any one from:
   - He's (often/always/very) tired
   - Has to get up early (in the morning/next day)

4. (a) He has little contact/does not spend a lot of time with (other) young people/people of his own age

   (b) Any two from:
   - He went to live at a classmate's/school friends house
   - He went to live in town
   - It lasted a month
   NB If there is an indication that it is not a simultaneous exchange, you will lose 1 mark

5. (a) He couldn't sleep/he did not sleep well/couldn't get to sleep/did not sleep much

   (b) Any one from:
   - He missed the quiet of the country(side)/the country(side) was quieter/it was noisier than the countryside
   - (He heard) (the) noise(s) in the street
   - (He heard) people going home (late)
   - (He heard) cars passing by

6. (a) Any two from:
   - Go out with friends(to the cinema/to see films)
   - Chat at the café(with friends)
   - Go to a club/go clubbing/the disco/stay out/come home/late **at the weekend**

   (b)
   - With biology department/teacher/biology trip
   - Studied/saw/watched/observed/examined/looked at (small) animals/creatures which lived on the river edge/bank/by the river side

7. (a) At a friend's house/at a friend's birthday/party birthday party

7. (b) Any two from:
   - She's interested in animals
   - She wants to be/become a vet
   - She's going/coming to spend a weekend at the farm

8.
   - Doesn't get on with the teachers
   - Has to do boring subjects/
     Finds (history/some) lessons boring

9. Any two from:
   - Works in a big shop/dept. store(at the weekend)
   - The work is not (too) hard/the work is easy
   - It's not well paid/bad pay
   - She doesn't make enough/can't afford to go out with friends (in the evening)

10.
   - She will have (a lot) **more** independence

   - She will have lessons/classes/subjects **which interest her**

   - She will meet (young) people **with the same interests/tastes**

# French Credit Level
# Reading 2004

1. (a) They protested/demonstrated/marched (in Paris)/took part in a demonstration/held a demonstration.

   (b) • (Two) **policemen** tried to / attempted to arrest / were arresting / arrested / apprehended / a burglar / robber / thief / catch a burglar
   • They were killed / murdered.

   (c) • 2 policemen/they/stopped a car/they tried to stop a car.
   • (The/a) **driver/motorist** shot (at) them / They were shot at/fired at by the **driver/motorist**.

2. (a) • Recruit / take on **3000** (new/extra/more) policemen / officers/recruit **3000** more
   • Provide / give them / distribute **bullet-proof** vests / jackets / waistcoats / body armour / clothing / protection

   (b) Public opinion supports/is with the police(men)/ it's what the public wants.

3. (a) • (Near/on) a/the motorway.
   • (Big) high **speed** / (very) **fast** / TGV / express / train / rail (link) **speed** train

   (b) One of:
   • Sparsely/not heavily populated/not a big population / few people live there.
   • Noise of planes / noise / planes / won't disturb (too) **many** people.

   (c) • Government has imposed its decision/made decision without discussion / debate / consultation / didn't give them a choice/the decision was made without consultation/ they were not asked.
   • (They don't want the) noise **and** pollution.

4. (a) Roissy and Orly (only) working / using / functioning at **half** their capacity / **half** full / used / they don't use **half** their capacity.

   (b) (About) 10 years

   (c) • (In that time) number of passengers will double / is doubling
   • Roissy and Orly can't cope / are incapable of coping with / absorbing / holding that increase.

5. (a) To alert / tell / inform the world about the (high) number / millions of children who work.

   (b) They have most of / the highest numbers of working children / these countries are the worst.

   (c) To help / aid / support / provide for / earn money for / sustain their families.

   (d) One of:
   • They work in agriculture/on the land / farming / on farms/in farming.
   • They gather / harvest / collect / pick tobacco / cocoa.

6. (a) Developing / Third World / under developed / poorly developed countries

   (b) They cost / earn less (than adults) / their wages are lower / they don't have to pay them as much (as adults) / adult wages.

   (c) They **make / produce / manufacture** clothes/outfits/shoes/carpets/rugs.

   (d) Stop employing / not to employ / take on / children (any more).

   (e) • The/their **families** / depend / are dependent on their money/need their money.
   • The **families** might **die** of hunger / starve to **death** (without the money they earn).

# French Credit Level
# Listening 2004

**1.** Any two of:
- She was born in Paris
- Spent /passed/lived (the first) **seven** years in **Algeria.**
- Her father was / is a diplomat.

**2.** Any one of:
- She is the youngest (of the family).
- She has **two big / bigger / older / elder** brothers.
- Her brothers are 7 and 9 years older than her.

**3.** Any two of:
- Speaking English / couldn't speak English (well)/trying to speak English
- (Understanding) the / their **French** accent
- Making / meeting / finding (new) friends

**4.** (a) The **summer** holiday(s) / break / vacation

(b) Any two of:
- (for) a (whole) month
- in (a huge / vast / big) forest(s)/wood(s)
- in a cabin / hut / lodge / chalet
- at / on / beside / by / to / near / around lake/loch
- 200km from Quebec

**5.** •  It/there was a (small) village **nearby / near the cabin**
- Everyone knew each other (well)
- There were **young** people OR people **of her age** / children **of her age**
- She improved / perfected her English / she could / had a chance to improve / perfect her English

**6.** (a) She (ice-)skated / went to the ice-rink / she learned to skate.

(b) She broke / fractured her leg.

**7.** (a) Any one of:
- She spent very little time there / in France (up to the age of 16)
- She was only in / visited France **twice** (when she was young)

(b) •  Her cousin's wedding / marriage
- Grandfather's death / funeral

**8.** Any two of:
- Her parents returned to France / Paris (two years ago) / her parents are (back) in France / Paris.
- Her father works in an office / in the suburbs/ outskirts of Paris.
- Her brothers (still) live / have stayed in Canada.

**9.** •  Her/one brother is married with 3 children.
- An/one/the other is unemployed / doesn't have a job.

**10.** (a) •  (Every day) he eats in the school canteen / dining-hall / café.
- Eats / has fast-food / take-aways / goes to a fast-food restaurant **two or three times a week**.

(b) Any one of:
- He will / could have **health** problems (in the future) / they don't want him to have health problems OR they are worried about his **health in the future** / (if he doesn't eat good food) he's risking his health.
- He doesn't eat healthily / properly / healthy food / proper food / right food.

**11.** Any one of:
- It's **not just** about diet / food/what you eat.
- Take **regular** (physical) exercise **as well**.
- Eat properly **and** take **regular** (physical) exercise

**12.** Any two from:
- Walking to school / go to school on foot (instead of going by car / getting a lift from dad / parents)
- Go to the gym OR exercise with friends / in a group.
- Take the bike when you go shopping/cycle to the shops.

# French Credit Level
# Reading 2005

1. **Georges**
anytime/whenever I want
OR when I am/feel ill/unwell/sick at school

   **Sarah**
there are/were still/another 10/10 more left

   **Vanessa**
I feel like smashing/breaking them/it
I want to break them

   **Pierre**
go into town alone/on my own/myself
OR stay out until midnight
stay out late
go into town until midnight

   **Jean-Luc**
are (standing) 20 m away/just metres/yards away
(standing) nearby

2. (a) Not free/allowed/permitted to/can't write/say
what they want/about certain things/
only allowed to write about certain things/can't
print certain things

   (b) *Any two of*
   • Fewer died/killed (in 2003) than in 2002
     OR
      25 of them/journalists died/killed (in
      2003) (which was fewer than in 2002)
   • (Acts of) violence/aggression (have/has)
     increased/were more numerous
   • 118 journalists/people are/were/have been
     put in prison/were imprisoned

   (c) • Armed groups/people
     Groups with weapons
   • (Acts of) violence/aggression (have/has)
     increased
   • (the) Government(s)

3. (a) In case they embarrass/upset/cause
governments problems/bother/
annoy/disturb/harm/trouble/ get in the way of
the government/ rulers of the country

   (b) • Defend reporters/journalist(s) (who are) in
     prison
   • Money for the families/helps the families
     of those who are dying/ have died/who
     have had someone killed
   • Help journalists/families of journalists
     who have fled/escaped the/their country

   (c) To sell (a collection of their) photos (to raise
   funds for RSF)
   OR
   (To run/start a campaign)
   To defend the freedom of the press

4. (a) Selling/a sales assistant for double
   glazing/double glazed windows
   From his sister's nephew

   (b) He lived near/right next to/beside (the/a
   stadium) where they trained/ training ground

4. (c) *One of*
   • He was a (very/rather/quite) good
     pupil/student/an excellent pupil
   • (Always/usually) got good marks (in most
     subjects)/was good at most of his subjects

   (d) His solo career didn't take off immediately/took
   (several/many) years/a long time/was slow to get
   going

   (e) He will never have to worry about money
   He will have enough money to last him till the
   end of his days/for all his life

5. (a) He has/had/he's bought a house in L.A.
   /there/in California/in the USA
   OR
   He spends a lot of time in California/America/
   there

   (b) There will be fireworks/ unforgettable
   (shows/spectacle)

   (c) Lots/many/most tickets are bought by British
   people
   British people buy most tickets
   Many British people go to see him.

   (d) *Any two of*
   • I've/he's had lots of girlfriends
   • He will have (more) girlfriends/ more of
     them in the future
   • (the) Government(s)
   • He can't/it's difficult to resist a
     pretty/beautiful/nice looking/lovely/
     attractive girl(s)/woman

# French Credit Level
# Listening 2005

1. • There was/he went to/he was at a music festival/fest/fair/fête (on Saturday)
   • There were (at least) 12 bands/orchestras/lots of dancers/lots of (people) dancing (in the main street/road)

2. *Any two of*
   • There were lots of people/there was a (large) crowd/he was in the crowd of spectators
   • He was pushed/jostled (from behind)
   • He fell
   • (he knew) it was serious
   • They/the hospital diagnosed a broken leg/he broke his leg

3. (a) he was in (a room/ward) with (lots of ) old/elderly/aged people

   (b) he is in (a room) with (3) people his own age/ the same age

4. *Any two of*
   • The meals aren't/the food isn't as good as at home/he gets better meals/food at home
   • There are dishes/meals/food/things/stuff he doesn't like (sometimes)/there are dishes he doesn't like
   • Mum brings him food/he phones his mum and she brings him stuff (he wants) (he chooses)/ he phones his mum for food/his mum brings him his meals

5. (a) The end of the week/at the weekend/in a few days time

   (b) Stay with his friend/Gérard/stay with a friend/ with someone else (who lives nearby)
   go to his friend/Gérard (for 4 days)

6. (a) Eleven years

   (b) *Any two of*
   • They/the boys/families lived in same street
   • They/the boys were/are the same age
   • They were/met in the same class (in primary school)

7. (a) *Any two of*
   • They met/saw each other every day
   • Went to school by bike
   • Ate lunch together/in school/in canteen/went to the canteen at midday/ate together in school/ ate in the canteen
   • Came home together/at same time

   (b) *Any one of*
   • They went to each other's houses (to play)/ played at each other's houses
   • He went to Marc's house or Marc came to his house
   • After dinner/tea/supper they played

8. (a) *Any two of*
   • Stayed/went to/up/in the mountains (for a month)
   • Did pony trekking/horse riding
   • Went (rock/mountain) climbing/mountaineering
   • Went water ski-ing
   • He went horse riding in the mountains

   (b) He/they got to know/met/there were (lots of young) people from all parts of France

9. • Different languages/(modern/foreign) language(s)/living language(s)
   • a chemist/pharmacist
   • a friend/pal for life

10. (a) *One of*
   • The house/life will be (very/a lot) quiet(er)/calm(er)/ tranquil/peaceful
   • There will be no/less/arguments/fights/ dispute

   (b) *Any two of*
   • There are (often) arguments/fights/disputes
   • He comes home (very/too) late during the week
   • He leaves his room messy/untidy/he never tidies/ cleans his room/the state of his room
   • He watches too much TV/he's always watching TV/he spends all his/a lot of/ time in front of TV/all he does is watch TV/how much TV he watches/he always has the TV on

# French Credit Level
# Reading 2006

1. (a) • Great/excellent/first rate/cool/top
      quality fantastic/super/sound/really good/the
      best/something else
   • Should/has to/must/ought to try it/give it a
      try/she should (try to) start smoking/she
      should do it

   (b) • Won't speak/talk to her (anymore/any
      longer/again)/will no longer speak to her/will
      refuse to speak to her/will stop speaking to
      her

2. (a) • **About/approx/almost/nearly** half of them/
      teenagers/young people/youth(s)/people
      smoke

   (b) One of
      • More (and more) of them (are beginning to)
        smoke
      • They start/are smoking younger/
        earlier/sooner/they're younger when they start

   (c) Any two of
      • Bad breath
      • Yellow fingers
      • (More) serious illness(es)/diseas(es)/become
        seriously ill/seriously bad health/disease(s)
        like cancer…

   (d) One of
      • Refusing to give smokers/smoking a positive
        image/they refuse to advertise smoking as a
        positive thing
      • Informing people of the (health) dangers of
        tobacco/smoking/they give out facts about
        how bad it is (for your health)

3. (a) • (Amount/weight of) **household/domestic**
        waste/rubbish/refuse/garbage/litter

   (b) (i) • Use less packaging/wrapping (like…)
       (ii) • Waste less paper/won't waste too
              much paper/save (more) paper/paper
              is going to waste

   (c) • To encourage customers/them/the
        French/people to buy/use goods which
        respect/are friendly to the environment/are
        environmentally friendly/which do not
        damage the environment
      • Re-use/recycle plastic bags

4. (a) One of
      • He wanted/wants to do something involving/
        with sciences/in the field of science(s)
      • He liked/likes/enjoys/enjoyed biochemistry
        and physics (at school)

4. (b) • He studied for 6 years/6 years of study (at
        college/university)
        OR
        He/you finish(es) studying (quite) late
        OR
        You don't finish until you are 23 (or older/
        more)/you need to be (over) 23 (or more)
        before you start/he was 23 **or more** when he
        became a pharmacist

   (c) • Hospital lab(s)
      • Drug companies/manufacturers of medicines/
        drug/medicine manufacturing/
        places where drugs are made

   (d) Any two of
      • He/one/you **has/have to** be interested in
        people
      • He/one/you **has/have to** get on well with
        (his) customers/clients/patients
      • They tell him/come to him with/about their
        **health/medical** problems
      • He/you explain(s) the/their prescription(s)

5. (a) • Fewer people use the post/less mail/post/
        fewer letters/less need for post
      • Less work/fewer jobs for postmen
        OR
        Job losses/unemployment for postmen/
        postmen made redundant

   (b) • Mobile (phone(s))/laptop(s)

   (c) • You/it need(s) chargers **and** a network/it
        needs charged **and** a network/it runs out of
        batteries and it needs a network

   (d) • Computers do all the work **in the future**/
        computers will do all the work (in the future)
        ….for/of men/man/humans
      • People will not become/get/be bored
      • People will be able to give (all) their
        time/have time to enjoy themselves/have
        fun/entertain themselves/leisure pursuits

# French Credit Level
# Listening 2006

1. •   We/they get on (well)
    OR
    we/they have a good relationship/rapport
    OR
    he has a good relationship/rapport with her
    OR
    they are (good) friends
    OR
    they are (very) close
    OR
    she gets on well with him/me

2. *Any two of*
    • We/they (would) (only) spend/spent a/one week here/there/in France/in the hotel/in July/in summer
    • Our/their main/principal/other holiday is/was in winter
    OR
    We/they spend two weeks/fifteen days skiing
    OR
    We/they spend two weeks/fifteen days in Switzerland
    OR
    We/they go/went skiing in Switzerland

3. *Any two of*
    • Lots to do for young(er) people/children/youth(s)/teenagers/adolescents
    • Theme park/fun park/amusement park
    • (You can go) horse-riding

4. *Any two of*
    • He's (very) good/gifted/talented (at sport(s)/it/them)
    • Plays team **and** individual sports
    OR
    He's in a/the sports team **and** does sport on his own
    • (He is/was) school swimming champion
    OR
    At school he's a/the champion swimmer

5. • Helped/worked in a club for/with (young) children/youngsters/kids
    OR
    Helped/worked in a club for 5–10 year olds
    • Spent **whole** day/time/holiday/week/fortnight in the open air/outside/doing outdoor activities
    OR
    Played/worked…

6. (*a*) • Not good/poor/rubbish/no use at/can't do Maths **and** French

    (*b*) *One of*
    • Not interested in working/sitting in an office/doing office work/sitting behind a desk

6. (*b*) (continued)
    OR
    Wouldn't like to/doesn't want to work/sit in an office/to do office work/to sit behind a desk
    • Must find a job where he'll be active
    OR
    (Wants) an active job/one

7. • She read/was enthusiastic about/liked **all sorts/kinds of** books/lots of **different** books
    • Sometimes forgot to/didn't/wouldn't come and eat (when/because she was reading/so she could finish her book)
    OR
    Sometimes forgot/mealtimes/didn't/wouldn't eat with the family

8. • Worked/helped/did work experience in local/town/municipal/council library
    OR
    worked/helped/did work experience in a/the library in July/in the holidays
    • Replaced the/a librarian (who was on holiday)

9. • To get information from the Internet
    • (Students/pupils/people/they come) to do research/prepare/revise/study **for exams**

10. (*a*) • He's a farmer/has/had/owns/owned/ran/works/worked on a (small) farm
    OR
    grew/produced/sold fruit/vegetables

    (*b*) • Transported/took produce/products/goods/stuff/it/fruit/vegetables **to market** (on Saturday mornings)

11. (*a*) • Treats her like an adult

    (*b*) *One of*
    • (Too/over) protective when she goes out/wants to go out
    • Doesn't understand/realise that she's no longer a child/that she's a grown up
    OR
    He thinks she's still a child

12. *Any two of*
    • They want to be independent
    • (They are/can be) influenced by others
    • (They can/could be tempted to) take/be involved in/be offered/do drugs
    OR
    (They can/could) drink **a lot/too much**

13. • They're (very) different (from each other)
    • What they will do (in life/in the future/as a job) does not worry/bother him
    OR
    As long as they get a job where they're happy/which they like